Living with Autism Spectrum Disorder

By Jeremy Tolmie

This book is dedicated to Dave Ray for without him I would not be where I am today.

Chapter 1

The symptoms of Autism

Defining Autism

Autism spectrum disorder (ASD) and autism are both general terms for a group of complex disorders of brain development. These disorders are characterized, in varying degrees, by difficulties in social interaction, verbal and nonverbal communication and repetitive behaviours.

Autism appears to have its roots in very early brain development. However, the most obvious signs of autism and symptoms of autism tend to emerge between 2 and 3 years of age. Both children and adults with autism typically show difficulties in verbal and non-verbal communication, social interactions, and leisure or play activities.

Autism Spectrum Disorder has specific diagnostic criteria outlined in the American Psychiatric Association's Diagnostic & Statistical Manual of Mental Disorders (DSM-IV-TR).

Who is Affected?

ASD occurs in all racial, ethnic, and socioeconomic groups, but are almost five times more common among boys than among girls. CDC estimates that about 1 in 68 children (2014 CDC) has been identified with an autism spectrum disorder (ASD).

Types of ASD
There are three different types of Autism Spectrum Disorders:

- **Autistic Disorder** ASD LEVEL 3 (ALSO CALLED "CLASSIC" AUTISM)
This is what most people think of when hearing the word "autism." People with autistic disorder usually have significant language delays, social and communication challenges, and unusual behaviors and interests. Many people with autistic disorder also have intellectual disability.
- **Asperger Syndrome ASD LEVEL 1**
People with Asperger syndrome usually have some milder symptoms of autistic disorder. They might have social challenges and unusual behaviors and interests. However, they typically do not have problems with language or intellectual disability.
- **Pervasive Developmental Disorder** – NOT OTHERWISE SPECIFIED (PDD-NOS; ALSO CALLED "ATYPICAL AUTISM") ASD LEVEL 2
People who meet some of the criteria for autistic disorder or Asperger syndrome, but not all, may be diagnosed with PDD-NOS. People with PDD-NOS

usually have fewer and milder symptoms than those with autistic disorder. The symptoms might cause only social and communication challenges.

Signs and Symptoms

ASDs begin before the age of 3 and last throughout a person's life, although symptoms may improve over time. Some children with an ASD show hints of future problems within the first few months of life. In others, symptoms might not show up until 24 months or later. Some children with an ASD seem to develop normally until around 18 to 24 months of age and then they stop gaining new skills, or they lose the skills they once had. A person with an ASD might:

- Not respond to their name by 12 months

- Not point at objects to show interest (point at an airplane flying over) by 14 months

- Not play "pretend" games (pretend to "feed" a doll) by 18 months

- Avoid eye contact and want to be alone

- Have trouble understanding other people's feelings or talking about their own feelings

- Have delayed speech and language skills

- Repeat words or phrases over and over (echolalia)

- Give unrelated answers to questions

- Get upset by minor changes

- Have obsessive interests

- Flap their hands, rock their body, or spin in circles

- Have unusual reactions to the way things sound, smell, taste, look, or feel

Prevalence of Autism

Autism statistics from the U.S. Centers for Disease Control and Prevention (CDC, April 2012) identify around 1in 68 American children as on the autism spectrum. Careful research shows that this increase is only partly explained by improved diagnosis and awareness. Studies also show that autism is five times more common among boys than girls. An estimated 1 out of 48 boys and 1 in 252 girls are diagnosed with autism in Canada.

Causes and Risk Factors

Scientist do not know all of the causes of ASDs. However, they have learned that there are likely many causes for multiple types of ASD. There may be many different factors that make a child more likely to have

ASD, including environmental, biologic and genetic factors.

- Most scientists agree that genes are one of the risk factors that can make a person more likely to develop an ASD.

- Children who have a sibling or parent with an ASD are at a higher risk of also having an ASD.

- ASDs tend to occur more often in people who have certain other medical conditions. About 10% of children with an ASD have an identifiable genetic disorder, such as Fragile X syndrome, tuberous sclerosis, Down syndrome and other chromosomal disorders.

- Some harmful drugs taken during pregnancy have been linked with a higher risk of ASDs, for example, the prescription drugs thalidomide and valproic acid.

- We know that the once common belief that poor parenting practices cause ASDs is not true.

- There is some evidence that the critical period for developing ASDs occurs before birth.

Social communication and interaction

A child or adult with autism spectrum disorder may have problems with social interaction and communication skills, including any of these signs:

- Fails to respond to his or her name or appears not to hear you at times

- Resists cuddling and holding, and seems to prefer playing alone, retreating into his or her own world

- Has poor eye contact and lacks facial expression

- Doesn't speak or has delayed speech, or loses previous ability to say words or sentences

- Can't start a conversation or keep one going, or only starts one to make requests or label items

- Speaks with an abnormal tone or rhythm and may use a singsong voice or robot-like speech

- Repeats words or phrases verbatim, but doesn't understand how to use them

- Doesn't appear to understand simple questions or directions

- Doesn't express emotions or feelings and appears unaware of others' feelings

- Doesn't point at or bring objects to share interest

- Inappropriately approaches a social interaction by being passive, aggressive or disruptive

- Has difficulty recognizing nonverbal cues, such as interpreting other people's facial expressions, body postures or tone of voice

Patterns of behaviour

A child or adult with autism spectrum disorder may have limited, repetitive patterns of behaviour, interests or activities, including any of these signs:

- Performs repetitive movements, such as rocking, spinning or hand flapping

- Performs activities that could cause self-harm, such as biting or head-banging

- Develops specific routines or rituals and becomes disturbed at the slightest change

- Has problems with coordination or has odd movement patterns, such as clumsiness or walking on toes, and has odd, stiff or exaggerated body language

- Is fascinated by details of an object, such as the spinning wheels of a toy car, but doesn't understand the overall purpose or function of the object

- Is unusually sensitive to light, sound or touch, yet may be indifferent to pain or temperature

- Doesn't engage in imitative or make-believe play

- Fixates on an object or activity with abnormal intensity or focus

- Has specific food preferences, such as eating only a few foods, or refusing foods with a certain texture

As they mature, some children with autism spectrum disorder become more engaged with others and show fewer disturbances in behaviour. Some, usually those with the least severe problems, eventually may lead normal or near-normal lives. Others, however, continue to have difficulty with language or social skills, and the teen years can bring worse behavioural and emotional problems.

When to see a doctor

Babies develop at their own pace, and many don't follow exact timelines found in some parenting books. But children with autism spectrum disorder usually show some signs of delayed development before age 2 years.

If you're concerned about your child's development or you suspect that your child may have autism spectrum disorder, discuss your concerns with your doctor. The symptoms associated with the disorder can also be linked with other developmental disorders.

Signs of autism spectrum disorder often appear early in development when there are obvious delays in language skills and social interactions. Your doctor may recommend developmental tests to identify if your child has delays in cognitive, language and social skills, if your child:

- Doesn't respond with a smile or happy expression by 6 months

- Doesn't mimic sounds or facial expressions by 9 months

- Doesn't babble or coo by 12 months

- Doesn't gesture — such as point or wave — by 14 months

- Doesn't say single words by 16 months

- Doesn't play "make-believe" or pretend by 18 months

- Doesn't say two-word phrases by 24 months

- Loses language skills or social skills at any age

No link between vaccines and autism spectrum disorder

One of the greatest controversies in autism spectrum disorder canters on whether a link exists between the disorder and childhood vaccines. Despite extensive research, no reliable study has shown a link between autism spectrum disorder and any vaccines. In fact, the original study that ignited the debate years ago has been retracted due to poor design and questionable research methods.

Avoiding childhood vaccinations can place your child and others in danger of catching and spreading serious diseases, including whooping cough (pertussis), measles or mumps.

Risk factors

The number of children diagnosed with autism spectrum disorder is rising. It's not clear whether this is due to better detection and reporting or a real increase in the number of cases, or both.

Autism spectrum disorder affects children of all races and nationalities, but certain factors increase a child's risk. These may include:

- **Your child's sex.** Boys are about four times more likely to develop autism spectrum disorder than girls are.

- **Family history.** Families who have one child with autism spectrum disorder have an increased risk of having another child with the disorder. It's also not uncommon for parents or relatives of a child with autism spectrum disorder to have minor problems with social or communication skills themselves or to engage in certain behaviors typical of the disorder.

- **Other disorders.** Children with certain medical conditions have a higher than normal risk of autism spectrum disorder or autism-like symptoms. Examples include fragile X syndrome, an inherited disorder that causes intellectual problems; tuberous sclerosis, a condition in which benign tumors develop in the brain; and Rett syndrome, a genetic condition occurring almost exclusively in girls, which causes slowing of head growth, intellectual disability and loss of purposeful hand use.

- **Extremely preterm babies.** Babies born before 26 weeks of gestation may have a greater risk of autism spectrum disorder.

- **Parents' ages.** There may be a connection between children born to older parents and autism spectrum disorder, but more research is necessary to establish this link.

Complications

Problems with social interactions, communication and behaviour can lead to:

- Problems in school and with successful learning

- Employment problems

- Inability to live independently

- Social isolation

- Stress within the family

- Victimization and being bullied

Prevention

There's no way to prevent autism spectrum disorder, but there are treatment options. Early diagnosis and intervention is most helpful and can improve behaviour, skills and language development. However, intervention is helpful at any age. Though children usually don't outgrow autism spectrum disorder symptoms, they may learn to function well.

The main signs of autism are differences in how autistic people communicate and interact with others.

Autism is a spectrum condition, which means that it affects people in different ways.

But most autistic people see, hear and experience the world differently from other people.

Although the signs of autism vary widely among children, young people and adults, there are 2 common characteristics:

- difficulties with social communication and interaction – autistic people may find it hard to join in conversations or to make friends

- repetitive behavior, routines and activities – such as fixed daily routines, repetitive body movements and a hypersensitivity to certain sounds

Autistic people may also be under- or oversensitive to certain sounds, lights, colours and other things, known as sensory sensitivity.

These signs are present over time and have a noticeable effect on daily life.

See a GP or health visitor if you notice any of the signs of autism in your child or you're concerned about your child's development.

You can also talk to your child's teacher or care worker.

If you're an adult and are concerned about signs of autism in yourself, talk to a GP.

Possible signs of autism in pre-school children

The signs given here do not necessarily mean your child is autistic. And autistic children may not show all the signs.

Spoken language
- delayed speech development (for example, speaking less than 50 different words by the age of 2) or not speaking at all
- repeating set words and phrases

- speech that sounds monotonous or flat
- communicating using single words, despite being able to speak in sentences

Responding to others

- not responding to their name being called, despite having a hearing test showing normal hearing
- rejecting cuddles initiated by a parent or carer (although they may initiate cuddles themselves)
- reacting unusually negatively when asked to do something by someone else

Interacting with others

- not being aware of other people's personal space, or being unusually upset by people entering their own personal space
- limited interest in interacting with other people, including children of a similar age
- not enjoying situations other children of their age enjoy
- preferring to play alone, rather than asking others to play with them
- difficulties using and understanding gestures, body language and facial expressions when communicating
- avoiding eye contact

Repetitive or unusual behaviour

- having repetitive movements, such as flapping their hands, rocking back and forth, or flicking their fingers

- playing with toys in a repetitive or unexpected way, such as lining blocks up in order of size or colour, rather than showing imaginative play

- preferring to have a familiar routine and getting very upset if there are changes to this routine

- having a strong like or dislike of certain foods based on the texture or colour of the food as much as the taste

- over- or under sensitivity to sensory stimuli, such as sounds, smells, colours and lights

Possible signs of autism in school-age children

The signs given here do not necessarily mean your child is autistic. And autistic children may not show all the signs.

Spoken language

- avoiding using spoken language

- speech that can sound monotonous or flat

- speaking in pre-learned phrases, rather than putting together individual words to form new sentences

- a tendency to dominate conversations with others, focusing on topics that are of particular interest to the child

Responding to others
- taking people's speech literally and finding it difficult to understand sarcasm, metaphors or figures of speech
- reacting very negatively when asked to do something by someone else

Interacting with others
- being less aware of other people's personal space, or being very upset by people entering their own personal space
- appearing to have little interest in interacting with other people, including children of a similar age, or having few close friends, despite attempts to form friendships
- not understanding how people usually interact socially, such as greeting people or saying goodbye
- finding it hard to adapt the tone and content of their speech to different social situations – for example, speaking very formally at a party then speaking to total strangers in a familiar way
- not enjoying situations and activities that a lot of children of their age enjoy
- rarely using gestures, body language or facial expressions when communicating

- avoiding eye contact

Unusual or repetitive behaviour

- repetitive movements, such as flapping their hands, rocking back and forth, or flicking their fingers

- playing in a repetitive or seemingly unimaginative way

- often preferring to play with objects rather than people

- developing a highly specific interest in particular subjects or activities

- preferring to have a familiar routine and getting very upset if there are changes to their normal routine

- having a strong like or dislike of certain foods based on the texture or colour of the food as much as the taste

Possible signs of autism in adults

The signs given here do not necessarily mean an adult is autistic. And autistic adults may not show all the signs.

Interacting with others

- not always understanding social "rules"

- understanding "personal space" differently
- feeling anxious or stressed in social situations
- finding it hard to judge "appropriate" interactions, such as being either too formal or too familiar
- finding it difficult to make friends and keep them
- lack of eye contact or too much

Communication

- speech may have a different stress or pitch
- use of repetition
- asking questions that other people might find inappropriate

Unusual or repetitive behaviour

- preferring or being reliant on routine
- feeling anxious or stressed at changes that may seem minor to other people
- having particular or very focused interests
- finding rituals helpful
- finding it hard to understand abstract concepts, such as time and choice

Autistic adults are more likely to have had problems staying in education or finding and staying in work.

Chapter 2

A little bit about me

Hi, my name is Jeremy Tolmie I am 37 years old and have Autism spectrum disorder Level 1.

I am a certified computer technician having graduated from Academy of Learning with my Computer Service Technician Diploma with honors.

I used to work for Literacy Central Vancouver Island as a computer technician. I refurbish donated computers that go to families with kids on welfare.

I used to live with my parents in a 500 SQF bachelor pad. They converted the carport into a living space for me. It has a walk-

in closet and a full bathroom. I just share the laundry room.

kitchen, and dining room.

I now live with a support worker who takes care of me and

cooks my suppers. He also is an advocate for me helping when

I need it. Like taking me to dr appointments and things like

that. The government pays him $716 a month room and board.

I get $417 from the government after paying the support

worker. I am working at the library putting books away. I

make $400 every 2 weeks doing that job. I have been doing it

for 3 years now.

I love computers, hockey, star trek, video games, alternative

music, crime tv shows, most movies except romantic comedies,

lord of the rings, harry potter, most fantasy and sifi books

movies and games, Netflix, apple products, reading, writing

and blogging, Facebook, cartoons, comics, and so much more.

my blogs are at

http://www.facebook.com/jeremytolmieauthorpage

http://livingwithautismbyjeremytolmie.blogspot.ca/

my personal Facebook page is

https://www.facebook.com/jeremy.tolmie

I am always up to making new friends on FB and getting new followers for my blogs. I am also always up to talking to people about what it has been like for me. Or about anything that they want to talk about. I am way more social on FB then I am in person that is why I love FB and am glad that it is around so that I can feel good about being social and giving me the time, I need to make conversations.

I am 18 months older than my brother but have not spoken to him in 17 years. I was adopted at 18 months and did not find out about him till 17 years ago. we met once and he is so much like me it is amazing. he does not look like me, but his mannerisms are so similar you would atomically know that we were brothers.

He got to grow up with my birth mother till she died when he was 14. I never got to meet her so all I have is what my brother said about her and what my blood grandmother said and what was in her medical file. she died from a brain tumour so that is how I found out about them at all. My biological grandmother got in touch with my parents to get me tested when I was 16.

the docs first DX was OCD at 16 a year latter they said PDD-
NOS then 6 months latter said ASD Asperger's syndrome.

It is just so frustrating to feel like you should be able to do all
the normal stuff that everybody else does and that it should
not be this hard or difficult. That there is no rhyme or reason
for how much anxiety you feel all the time. That it should not
be this hard to talk to people and keep friends. It really is hard
to deal with sometimes. I just wish the good days would out
way the bad days once in a while.
I hate when people ask how I feel. I have no freaking idea how
I feel so stop asking me this please and thank you. I could not
tell you or anyone how I am felling at any given time. I might
be able to tell you if it is a really strong emotion that I am
feeling but otherwise I have no clue.

I love music and have loved music since the first time I herd it.
I love singing to music, dancing to it, listening to it. any thing
with music is a passion of mine.

I calm down drastically when listening to music so when ever I get upset or am starting to have a meltdown, I grab my iPod and plug in the ear phones and play some music and it calms me right down in no time.

I did not start to read for fun till I was 18 and my parents bought me the first harry potter book. Till then I thought reading was just a waste of time and would have nothing to do with it.

Since then I have become a big-time reader and have read more than 50 books for fun.

I really love audio books and own more then 100 of them. I listen to them almost every day as I take the bus to and from work.

I am 5 foot 8 and weigh 155 pounds. I have next to no muscle tone in any of my body even less in my left arm which is pretty much useless. Thank god I am right handed because I can not use my left hand for any thing except typing and holding onto utensils. I can not move my left hand to cut food, so I hold the fork in it while I use my right to cut the food then take the fork in my right hand to eat with.

I cannot even move it to print with or catch with or any thing. It is so annoying.

When they test my academic skills, it shows that I have grade 2 age 7 writing, grade 4 age 9 spelling, grade 6 age 11 reading and grade 9 age 13 math skills. That was done 20 years ago when I was 17.

I am on clonazepam, divalproex, olanzapine, and abilify. The clonazepam is for my anxiety, the divalproex is my mood stabilizer, the olanzapine is my anti-psychotic, and the abilify is for the behaviour issues and helps with my meltdowns.

I was never medicated for ADHD. I was for the OCD symptoms and it was a nightmare. For me anti-depressants caused me to get many times worse.

I found turn based computer games to help a lot. Like civilization and games like that. They are educational and fun.

I always knew that I was different from other kids my age, but I never really thought of myself as having more than just a mild learning disability. So, it was not really that hard or difficult for me, but I think it was for my parents to see how I was treated by the other kids. I had a couple good friends and whenever I lost a friend, I usually found one or more to replace him with. I am still getting used to all of the symptoms and more seem to crop up or get worse every year.

Man, kids get it good these days. I never had any OT, PT, ST or stuff like it when I was a kid. I never had an aid worker or got any treatments. I guess it helps to get the DX early not like me starting at 17. That is way too late to be of much good. I had to do all the regular classes and courses. I had to fend for myself. Teachers never paid me the siltiest bit of attention. I never got any help from teachers to teach me anything. I had to teach myself how to do everything. I was expected to do everything a regular kid has to do at each stage of the game. The problem is that I never told anyone that I really could've used some help.

I really hate September and October. September always reminds me of going back to school and that meant a new teacher and new classroom to try to remember. I hatted going back to school. with in a week or two I would be fine I just hatted the going back part not the school part. I did not mind school so much as the change in routine. October is thanksgiving up here in Canada plus I have my moms and my grandma's birthdays and Halloween to deal with. It is just too much to deal with in a shot period of time that's all. Christmas and new years were not much better for me also. I never get any sleep Christmas eve. I think it goes back to when I was 5 and I was determined to catch Santa in the act of putting out the presents. I stayed up all night and caught my parents in the act. that was the end of the illusion of Santa for me.

There are not that many disabled people That I get to see every day. and the average tantrum I see is from a preschooler not getting what he wants from his parents.

I am a very independent person, so I see a lot more melt downs than my parent's foo.

I hate speaking in public it gives me a total meltdown every time I have to do it. I am not all that successful yet.

I think of all the crazy things I asked for for Christmas and my birthday. Like a horse, dirt bike, go kart, hover craft, trip to space, a pet t-rex. compared to some Like a new game or book or comic or upgrade to my computer. Or even a dog or cat seems small compared with some of the stuff I thought up for myself.

Most of my dreams come true for me. I am always having moments where I feel like I have already done them before and then I realize that I had a dream of doing exactly the same thing. I think that my whole life has already been planed out and I am just going along for the ride. I also have major anxiety issues and have a hard time adjusting to any change period. The start of school was very hard on me and I still get upset come September because of the start of the school year

When I was 12, we moved, and it was really hard on

me. I did not say anything to my parents about how hard it was. It took me 3 years to get adjusted to the new house and location. I acted really bad for those 3 years and got into a lot of trouble. I skipped 2 months of school with out my parents knowing till one of the teachers bumped into them at the grocery store and asked if I was alright because I had missed the last 2 months of school.

I also racked up $500 in long distance phone charges in one-month phoning movie studios and threading to sue them for movies that used names that I had thought of using. It was a really bad time in my life, but it did get better.

I wouldn't share with anyone it did not matter who they were. My parents kept having to tell me that I had to learn to share my stuff. I got over it eventually, but it did take a very long time to learn the art of sharing.

I was 17 when I got the DX of Asperger's syndrome

ASD. So, for me I would have liked to have known

much sooner than that. So that I could have had the

proper support in school.

I look, act, and seem very much like my blood

brother and I only got to see him once 17 years ago.

It was really freaky because we never grew up

together any, yet we are so much alike. He has the

same mannerisms, body language, speech patterns

and everything. It makes you wonder how much

nurture has to do with it or if it is mostly nature. The genetic

code that binds you together is stronger than anything on the

planet.

I watch crime TV shows and medical dramas. I

play virtual hockey games and watch hockey on

TV. I blog about what it was like growing up as

me. I read fantasy books and listen to their

audio books. I play strategy games on the computer and

fiddle with the computer to try and keep it in perfect

working order. That is what I do these days to make me

happy.

I played the drums, piano, and trombone and

got good at each one of them.

I have had several girl friends over the years. All

this having ASD. So, it is possible to live a semi

normal life. Hang in their it does get better. I

think the only one that should be called a

expert on ASD is someone who has ASD and

is able to talk about what it is like to have it.

You can ask me anything and I will try to answer it. I can not answer questions that I have not been asked.

Whenever I find a post that goes into something that I have knowledge in I comment on it and post the comment on my blog if it is worth while. I think everybody should benefit from my experiences

I was 17 when I got my first DX of Asperger's Syndrome, so my parents never put any limitations on me either. I tried every sport in the book till I found golf and bowling that I am good at. I know lots of people with ASD that live a pretty normal lives on their own and I am living a pretty normal life, so I think anything is possible.

you would think that someone would have noticed something was wrong and told my parents about it. But nope no one did, and it was just a fluke of my birth mom dyeing of a brain tumour and for me to get checked out that I even got the DX of ASD when I did.

I like people to know that I am autistic so that they can see the other side of it. I wear a hoodie that says I wear blue for autism awareness.

Most people think of autism as being the classic aloof form and don't realize how varied the disorder is.

My mom had to become a stay at home mom because every time she tried to drop me off at daycare I would start crying and throwing a tantrum till she stopped trying. The daycare people said after a week that they could not handle me because of the crying and tantrums that I would through. she took me to our pediatrician, and he said because I had come from foster care and was adopted that I was having abandonment issues and that it would not get better any time soon and that she should stay at home with me and be my own day-care provider. so, she did till I was 12 and then she went back to work.

I did do some pre-school, but I just hid under a table and did not partake in anything and would have nothing to do with anyone, so she gave up on that after a couple of months and just kept me at home till I was old enough to start kindergarten.

I think it is a big mistake to get rid of the Asperger's DX because without it in their most of us will not get a proper DX and will not get the services or support we deserve.

I would have been DXed as PDD-NOS which is what they were wanting to push on me but for one nero doc that said it was Asperger's.

Chapter 3

My earliest memories

The first thing that I can remember is being in my crib at night. There is a light shining under the door to my room. The door is closed and the lights in my room are off. I am trying to sleep lying on my back with a brown teddy bear in my arms. I hear my name said from my mother, which is in the dinning room down the hall from my room. It wakes me up and I try to hear the rest of the conversation about me but cannot make out what is being said so I try to go aback to sleep.

The second thing that I can remember is trying to walk with both of my parents holding one of my hands. My mom was holding my right hand and my dad was holding my left hand. I was not wearing glasses at the time and could not see my own two feet let alone anything else, so I kept tripping over my feet.

My parents would try and get me walking whenever they could, and I just kept tripping over my feet and they could not understand that it was because I could not see anything.

The third thing that I can remember is sitting right underneath the TV with my nose almost touching the screen. I did this every day till I got glasses and could see what was on the TV.

I was three years old when my parents finally took me to an eye doctor to get my eyes tested. I ended up having 400/20 vision in my left eye and 200/20 in my right eye. I ended up also having lazy eye in my left eye. I wore an eye patch on my right eye to strengthen up my left eye. Plus, from that point forward I had to ware glasses. I was considered legally blind without my glasses.

I started pre-school that year also, but I spent most of the time hiding under the tables instead of playing with the other children. It was in a church near ware we were renting at the time and had a grate playground.

My parents also used to take me to the local elementary school to use their playground. I used to love the swings their and the sandbox.

In the house we were renting we had a young family living in the basement with a little girl who I used to play with

We lived in a apartment before renting the house but I do not remember anything about that.

I got a ear infection in my right ear when I was two that was not caught till it was too late so I am partially hearing impaired in that ear.

When my parents moved from Brandon Manitoba to Nanaimo BC it was one of the hottest summers on record. We left the middle of August 1984 to have a new start in a new city where the weather was much nicer then that of the prairies.

On the way I got a bad case of heat stroke and had to be taken to the hospital in Kamloops BC. My parents had to give me cold showers and popsicles to get me rehydrated and drop my temperature.

We were taking different cars when we got to the ferry. My dad was in the moving van and my mom and me were in the car. We were able to get on the ferry but my dad with the moving van did not. He had all the information about where we were going once the ferry landed. We had all the money with us so he could not buy anything.

When the ferry landed my mom just found a place to park and we waited for my dad with the moving van to come on the next ferry.

My mom got very sick with the flue latter that day, so my dad had to unload everything from the moving van into the new apartment by himself up two sets of stairs. While me and my mom laid down and had a nap.

We went to Disney world in Orlando Florida the winter before moving to Nanaimo bc. I do not remember much of that trip. Also, on that trip we went to Mexico where I do remember being on a beach with lots of Mexican little kids rubbing my hair because they had never seen red hair before.

I had my second birthday in Mexico at some time share resort that my parents had. I do not remember much about that either.

When I was two, I got the Japanese measles and got very sick, but I survived and built up a good resistance to the measles.

Chapter 4

School Years

I never played with any of the kids when I was in Pre School or kindergarten. I just found a nice place by my self to play with the toys. I loved trains back then and got to go on some train rides across the country, which I really loved. They had a wooden train set that you could put together and take apart the tracks and put them in al sorts of different patterns I would spend hours doing that. Taking them apart and putting them back together in a different way.

By the time I was 10 I could not participate properly because I could not get enough oxygen to my brain and muscles.

 If I did any serious exercise I would pass out and it would take me several minutes before I would even wake up. A couple hours to fully recover from it. So, I stopped participating with any effort in PE. Which lowered my grades to C-.

I did not make my first friend till a kid down the road showed up and started talking to me about him self and how much he loved planes trains and big equipment. I made a friend in no time and that was when I was 4 years old. My second friend I made was a referral from him so one day at school he introduced this other kid to me and that was when I was 6 and in grade 1. So latter that day the kid asked me if I wanted to be friends with him, so I said sure.

My friendship with the first friend ended when I was 16 but it was on the way out since I was 10. When I made friends with a new kid at school my first friend got really jealous and it hurt out friendship hard.

My friendship with my second friend ended when he turned 12. He wanted to be with the cool kids, and I was not one of them so we went our separate ways and have not seen each other since.

The third friend ended when he turned 13 the same old story, he was too good to be friends with me, so we went our separate ways and have not seen each other since.

I Had found two boys 2 years younger than me that became my friends once I started grade 8. So, for that year I had two friends, but it did not last one moved away at the end of the school year and the other wanted cooler friends his own age.

When I started grade 9, I met my BFF who just lives less than a block away. He is disabled himself, so it is a good matchup. I don't know what his disability is. It has something to do with having an extra x chromosome but still being male.

We have been friends ever since then and keep in touch on a regular occasion. He is married now but is unable to have kids. His wife has ADD so they are good together.

A new kid moved in right behind our house when I turned 12 and their boy way 13 and he was the worst thing that could have ever happened to me. The moment the boy saw me he new that I was disabled and would be easy to beat up and take advantage of. He would trip me, push me, hit me, spit on me, and ram my head into the ground. AND this was a daily experience for me for the second half of grade 6. I was terrified of going to school and more terrified trying to get home again.

My parents went to talk to his parents, but his parents said it way me hurting him and not the other way around.

My parents went to the police and they said till there is serious injury caused they can not get in involved.

So, my parents put the house up for sale and we moved away to a small island with ferry service to the city that we had just sold from.

So, I went to a new school for grade 7 on a small island where they do not take kindly to the city folk. I had no friends and the kids there was being as miserable to me as they possibly could be.

The pushed me, hit me, spit on me, body checked me, sandwiched me and every possible thing to make me unwelcome their.

During recess I used to stand in a corner by myself and try not to get anybody's attention so that they would just leave me alone.

At lunch I would just try and find a quiet place by myself to eat my lunch in peace with out being called names or having my lunch splashed on me.

Both my parents were working full time, so they had no idea how bad it was for me or what was going on at school.

It got so bad that I just started not going to school and staying home sick. My voice had dropped by then so I would call in sick pretending to be my dad.

It worked to for more than a month I did not go to school. Till one day one of the teachers from the school bumped into my parents at the grocery store and asked after my health about why I had missed so much school.

That was the end of my staying at home from school. So, I put on a brave face and got the rest of the year out of the way as quickly and quietly as I could.

I always had trouble asking to go to the washroom especially in school. I would hold it at all cost so as not to disturb the class. That meant that I was not always successful and would do it in class. Most of that was caused by the teachers that got so fed up with people asking to go when they did not need to go just for an excuse to leave class and so no pee breaks were allowed during class. You had to wait till break time. I could not hold it that long sometimes. It went on like this till grade 7 when they finely put a note in my file that I can leave the classroom at any time without asking.

I hatted every second I had to spend in high school and the bus rides were nightmarish. Most of the time the other students would not even let me sit down. the bus driver did not care he would drive to the locations he was told to. did not matter to him if I was sitting or not.

I had to take 2 busses and 2 ferries each day to high school. What a nightmare. I did not even have a worker I had to figure everything out on my own. and high school is the worst because you now have 4 or 5 different classes each day and each day they are at a different time.

And then half way through the year they do it all over again with 4 or 5 new classes to do for the rest of the year. That can be up to 10 different classroom and teachers to remember over the school year. I did not even bother to use the lockers they assigned me I could not ever remember the combination for it and it changed every year. Not to mention having a second locker in the gym's locker room with a different lock combo to try to remember. Those were the worst years of my life and I am glad never to have to relive them ever again.

I was a 2.1 GPA student all through school and high school and did not even graduate from high school. I only completed grade 10 I drooped out in grade 11 because of all the problems with the meds that I was on. I never was on the honor roll or even on the honorable mention list.

Once i went to collage I became a 4.00 GPA and got on the Deans list and graduated with honors.

I first went into

 a Employment and life skills vocational program for people with disabilities for 2 years and then went into the Computer

Service Technician Diploma program for 1 year after that.

I got a 4.00 GPA and on the Deans list and graduated with honors from both of the programs that I did. So that says that when I do a course that I like and am good at I really can excel at it and ace it like no other can.

So, if your kid is fairly high functioning but did not do well in school does not mean that collage is out of the question. you just have to find the right courses to take that will make them excel at them.

Chapter 5

Most asked questions

1. Why do people with autism talk so loudly and
   weirdly?

For me I think that I have to talk loudly so that I can be
over heard by the people around me. My parents always
had to tell me as a kid to tone It down and talk softly. As
for my voice being weird it is the only way I know how
to talk it is a monotone voice for sure and a deep voice
too boot. I tend to talk to myself a lot of the time and it is
either really soft or really loud. I think it is because of all
the sounds in our minds that we are trying to talk over.
Plus all the music that constantly plays in our minds
sometimes it is the same song for hours on end.

2. Why do you ask the same questions over and over
   again?

Well for me it was time that I used to ask over and over
again till my parents got me a watch so that I would stop
asking that particular question. On other questions it is
because I forget that I have already asked that question. I
have a hard time with short term memory especially
verbal answers and any verbal commands. Even if I
repeat it in my head right after being told I still might
forget what the answer was.

3.	Why do you echo questions back at the asker?

Well for me when I was a kid I would do this for one to give me time to come up with an answer and two so that I know what the question is so that I give a proper answer. These days I do this in my head so that it does not bother people as much I still do it but no one knows that I do it.

4.	Why do you speak in that peculiar way?

All people with autism do speak in a way that regular people properly find unusual. Normal people can do a conversation in real time while people with autism cannot do that. We have to play what you are saying to us in our minds than think about what we want to say and then try and say it but sometimes our mind works too fast and we forget what we want to say or what you have said and we come out with bits and pieces of what we really wanted to say.

5.	Why do you take ages to answer questions?

Well as I stated above we have to repeat what you have asked us in our mind and then we have to think about what we want to say and that can take some time and then we say it. If you keep asking questions to us even if it the same one we have to start the process all over again.

6.   Why can you not have a proper conversation?

Well for me I find it very difficult to have conversations with people. I find it very hard to come up with things to talk about. Small talk is the hardest thing in the world for me to do and I don't have a clue of how to do it or where to begin. Sometimes I do not to badly especially if I know the person well and feel comfortable around them. I know to regular people small talk and conversations come second nature to you but to me I just don't know how to do it and do it very badly usually. I clam up and don't speak at all most of the time. I met up with another autistic person the other day and we barely said anything to each other. We went out for coffee one time and the other time we went for a walk and both times were very awkward. I wish I was better at this and this is one of the biggest barriers I have to a normal life. If I could get rid of one aspect of autism it would be this.

7.   Why don't you make eye contact when you are
     talking?

Well if I did I would not be taking in anything that you were telling me. In order to fully absorb your talking to me I have to focus all my energy on taking in all the words you are saying replaying them in my mind and coming up with suitable answers to your conversation. If I was to look you in the eye I would not be taking in a word you were saying as all my attention would be on your eyes. On the shape the color the whiteness and every detail of your eyes and face for that matter. I would be more then useless in talking back to you about what you are talking to me about. I do try to give eye contact without actually giving eye contact. Sometimes I can fool people into believing that I am giving eye contact.

8.   Do you prefer to be on you own?

Most people believe that people with autism want to be on their own but that is not the case at all. We desperately want to be with people on a small scale like with a friend or with our parents or roommates. But there is this misconception that we want to be on our own. I do like my own time most of the time but there is times that I really want to be around other people for the conversations and to listen to them speak to us and tell us stories or how their day went. Every time my roommate brings his girlfriend over for a visit I spend as much time as I can around them to pick up how to be with people and get in on the conversations. I love these times when she comes over. She spends the night every Thursday and I get a real pleasure out of her and my roommates company.

9.	Why do you ignore us when we are talking with you?

I used to work in retail and had this problem many time's where I would not realise that the customer was talking to me when I was doing some work. I got in trouble on several occasions because of this. One time there was this customer that kept saying in ever increasing volume HELLO! And I did not realise that she was trying to get my attention. At the time I was restocking the shelves and did not know that she was talking to me. I thought she was on the phone and was trying to get the attention of the person on the other end of the phone. Once I realised she was talking to me it was too late and she requested to have another staff member assist her as she thought I was deliberately ignoring her. When I am doing a task I cannot switch to talking to a person right away. It takes me a minute to adjust my thinking. If she had said excuse me or pardon me or anything else other then hello I would probably turned around and asked how I may help you today.

10. Why are your facial expressions so limited?

We don't know how to show our emotions on our faces as much as normal people show their emotions on their faces. We have a hard time reading other people's facial expressions and so we have a hard time with our own facial expressions. We do have expressions like if we are really happy or angary or exited or other really big emotions you can defiantly tell that we are experiencing those emotions.

11. Is it true you hate being touched?

For me unless it is a big rough and tough hug from someone that is close to me then yes I hate being touched. It hurts me when people touch me and makes me unconfutable to be touched by people that are not close to me. I hate when people try to give me a hug without my permission or even a hand shake can be uncomfortable.

12. When you are on one of your highs what is going through your mind?

For me if I am flapping my hands or acting really excited for no apparent reason for it it is because I have remembered something that made me happy or some book that I really enjoyed reading. Also some image that made me laugh or some song that I really enjoyed listening to. I have things pop into my mind at random that can make me laugh at inappropriate times or squeal like a pig. I am really into the hand flapling when I get excited.

13. What are your flashback memories like?

For me when I have a flashback memory it is as real to me as if I had just experienced it in real life. My dreams seem so real and frighting to me that I can not sleep sometimes because of them. I wish that they were not so vivid as I seem to have mostly bad memories playback in my mind over and over again. I had such a terrible childhood that the memories were horrendous.

14. Why don't you do what your told right away?

For me I need to process what you told me to do think about how I would go about doing it and then tell myself to go ahead and do it. It takes time to do all of that as I have to repeat your instructions in my mind before I can even begin to think about what I am going to do to get the job done. I will eventually get to it but it will take a bit of time.

15. Do you hate it when we make you do things?

For me I do hate It when I am made to do things as it is out of my comfort zone and as such makes me really nervous about how I will do at it. I was made to do five pin bowling for special Olympics last year and I hatted every minute of it. I got heartburn from it every time I had to go and I did not enjoy myself at all. This year I picked what I wanted to do and so I think it will go much smoother.

16. What is the worst thing about having autism?

The fact that you never notice how miserable we are with it. We just want to be normal and have a friend, a partner, children, a house, the things you take for granted and we will probably never have. I would give it all up to have that life where I get to live on my own and live a normal life. I think it is hardest not having many friends and not being able to continue on a conversation as easily as you do. I find it hard that I am sad and depressed most of the time because I cannot have the life that I wish I could. I work part time but that only pays me minimum wage so I don't get enough money to live on my own.

17. Would you like to be normal?

I don't know if I would or not like to be normal. I would like to have normal conversations and be able to give eye contact and live on my own and do the things I would like to do but probably never will. Like travel and go do places by myself. I would like to have a partner and have children and watch them grow up and become upstanding members of society. But I would not be me without it and it has helped me a lot at work because I am such a perfectionist that I do a wonderful job and my boss has nothing but good things to say about me.

18. Why are you too sensitive or insensitive to pain?

For me I am really sensitive to pain and am in pain all the time. It has to do with how our senses work and how our brain works interprets that information. For me as long as I can remember I have been in what to me is intense pain all over my body. Especially my knees, ribs, back, neck, and feet. For some their brain just does not feel any pain at all I often wish what it would feel like to live that life. For me though it is a hard time and pain meds have no effect. Nor does physio therapy, chiropractors or any other treatment that I have tried to do. I don't know exactly why I feel so much pain but I do know that I sure wish that I did not feel so much pain. It makes it hard to know when something is wrong and sending real pain. Or if it is just this phantom pain.

19. When you look at something what do you see first?

For me I see all of the little details of everything that I am looking at. Like when it is snowing I can make out every little snowflake that is falling to the ground. I see everything there is to see all at once. Plus I can remember all the details of what I see as far back as I can remember and I can remember everything right back to me in my crib so it is a lot of memories and images that I remember. I love how my mind works in that fashion because I can remember things from when I was really little. But it is a curse to because I can remember every thing that was bad that happened to me also.

20. Is it difficult to pick out appropriate clothing?

For me it is a little difficult as my body temperature does not work like normal peoples does. In the summer I still wear long sleeve shirts and full-length pants. As heat does not mean much to me as I am always cold. In the winter I tend to not wear enough warmth clothing and do not wear gloves or mites. I do wear my winter parka and a took if it is really cold out. But if it is above freezing I just wear a baseball hat. I don't find that I am too out of sync with what to wear but it probably looks weird to some especially in the summer.

21. Do you have a sense of time?

Well for me I have a terrible sense of time and have to constally check my watch to see what time it Is and make sure I leave work on time. If I did not have my watch or phone with me I would be at a loss of what time it is.

22. Why are your sleep patterns all messed up?

Well for me I don't need much sleep and I don't get much sleep. I wake up often and don't get back to sleep very quickly. I usually just get up when I wake up and listen to some music or play some games with the sound muted. I don't know why I don't need much sleep but I never have needed much sleep. I usually go to bed at a decent our but end up getting up really early.

23. Why do you like spinning?

I like spinning and watching things spin because it calms me and is a lot of fun to do. I have a computer chair that I like to spin in all the time. Spinning is a great relief and a great way to get grounded.

24. Why do you line up things?

For me the lining up of things is a way to organise things. As a kid I would line up my cars, toys, blocks, Legos, books, DVDs, CDs, and anything else I can line up. It makes me feel good that I have everything in its right place and can find it if I need it. Too this day I line things up so that I can find them. I also alphabetises my books, movies, music. Games and anything else that I can do it to.

25. Do you like commercials on tv?

For me I do like commercials on tv as they are short and I can memorise them and repeat them back to people. I like to do that as it gives me something to talk about. I think it is the fact that they are so short and easy to remember that makes me like them so much.

26. What kind of tv programs do you like to watch?

At this stage in my life I like to watch drams like grey's anatomy, crime shows like NCIS, I am not much into watching comedy or 30 minute shows. I prefer the hour long shows with a good story to them and a good cast of characters. When I was a kid I liked shows like arther, power rangers, star trek, anything on Disney channel. I liked sesame street, mr rogers, the big giant and shows like that. I used to get up a 6 and watch the early morning cartoons that would be on till 9.

27. Why do you memorise bus schedules and the like?

Well for me I like the fixed nature of the times that the buses come and go. I love numbers as a general rule and have done some pretty amazing things with numbers like figuring out how many nano seconds there would be if you lived to 100 years of age. I had a blast with that one and you would not even believe how big a number that is. I did it for fun and there is 100 nano seconds in a millisecond, 100 milliseconds in a second, 60 seconds in a minute. Well you get the idea anyway and it was a blast doing it.

28. What do you feel about running races?

I can do 150 feet sprints and 300 feet sprints but not much more then that. I did some of the sprints in races and won each and every one of them but when I attempted to run a mile ling race I came in second to last. So I am good at sprinting but bad at long distances.

29. Why do you enjoy going out for walks so much?

Well for me I love to walk anywhere even in my room or in the house I am almost always walking. I can think better when I am walking and it calms me down. I think I like going for walks so much is that I cannot stop moving most of the time. I can sit and watch tv or play my games but if I am not doing one of those two things I am walking.

30. Do you enjoy your free time?

For me I need my free time most defiantly to recharge my energy and get myself back to able to be with other people. I like to have my free time to play my games, watch tv, read my books and do things that I like to do.

31. Why don't you do what you are supposed to do even after being told many times?

For me it is that my brain just does not register that I should be doing something. Like putting the bananas away when they are on the counter, getting the sink ready to wash the dishes before supper instead of waiting till after supper, taking out the trash, and recycling, cleaning the house and things like that. I know deep down what I am supposed to do but for some reason I just can not seem to get myself to do it.

32. Why are you obsessive about certain things?

Well for me it is because I want to know about something or that I really want to get into something. Like I want to play a certain game and will play it for hours or even days at a time without sleeping or eating or anything. I do this quite often and start talking non stop about my obsession to anyone who will listen to me.

33. Why can you never stay still?

For me it is the fact that I just want to keep moving mostly walking for rocking or pacing or standing and moving around a little bit. I am always moving and I can only stay put for short periods of time. I like to be in motion it is comforting for me to be in motion and calms me down. I think if I tried to stay put for too long I would start to fidget and get antsy.

34. Do you need visual schedules?

For me I do not need them nor would I want them as things can change and if I had a visual schedule I would not like it if things did not go according to the schedule. I would have a complete melt down if we did not follow it to the letter. So no I do not need one nor want one.

35. What causes panic attacks and melt downs?

For me I get a panic attack or melt down if things don't go the way I thought they would go. Or if I had too much social contact or sensory overload. Also for me at work I tend to have lots of melt downs because I did not take my break at the right time or did not do enough work or did not sing in or out on time or did not do my job to my standards.   It starts at work and by the time I get home I am in full melt down mode and it takes me most of the rest of the day to recover from it.

36. What are your thoughts on autism yourself?

For me being on the milder side of the spectrum I really find it a hard thing to live with as I know I should be able to do all the things normal people do but just cannot do them. I think it is a hard place to be in if you are non-verbal and have sever issues I can see how that would be even harder to handle for the person and the caretaker. If there was a cure would I take it probably not now if you could selectively pick and choose which parts to get rid of then I would be more then glad to use it and get rid of the sensory issues and conversational issues but the rest I would not want to get rid of. I would not be me without them and I like who I am for the most part and I am in a good place for the most part now. I think that as doctors get educated they will find that there are a lot of people with autism that are not diagnosed for one reason or another. I was 17 when I got my diagnoses of Asperger's Syndrome and it made perfect sense to me of why I was the way I was and why things were so hard for me and why other kids and people treated me the way that they did. I think if I had known about it when I was a little kid I would have gotten the services that I needed and things would have been much better for me. But you cannot go into the past and fix things the way they should have been fixed. So I think I would not give up on me or anyone with autism of any kind as there is so much potential to get out of them. I know I will have a good life and things are looking up for me,

Chapter 6

My medical issues

I get meltdowns and shutdowns quite frequently but since my med change 2 months ago it has gone away. My meltdown is a little bit different than what happens to most people. I become agitated and cannot give eye contact plus I become non-verbal and have a hard time answering questions and also get fixated on dirt on my hands and on anything else. I don't through tantrums or slam doors or yell, scream, or do any of the normal stuff that usually goes along with a meltdown. I do have normal meltdowns sometimes, but they are rare and few and far between.

A meltdown is where a person with autism or Asperger's temporarily loses control because of emotional responses to environmental factors. They aren't usually caused by one specific thing.

Triggers build up until the person becomes so overwhelmed that they can't take in any more information. It has been described as feeling like a can of cola that has been shaken up, opened and poured out, emotions flowing everywhere.

They can look like a common or garden tantrum, but unlike tantrums, meltdowns can't be stopped by giving the person their own way.

Dependent on the cause of meltdown, it may be best to help the person leave the situation they find distressing. Everyone is different but some say that what they need to recover from a meltdown is being left alone in a place where they feel safe, listening to music, having a bath or sleeping.

After a meltdown the person often feels ashamed, embarrassed, and very tired.
As a parent to a child with autism, you're probably no stranger to meltdowns. You're also well aware that changes in routine can trigger or exacerbate meltdowns. That's why the summer can be particularly trying for both kids with autism, and their parents. During a sensory meltdown, children with special needs have very little control over their behavior. They may scream, break things, attack others and even try to hurt themselves. While it's painful to see your child lose control for seemingly no reason, meltdowns help you understand when your little one is experiencing sensory overwhelm. As a parent, it's essential that you learn to recognize the signs of a meltdown so you can keep your child safe and help them regain control and composure. Perhaps what's most terrifying about a sensory meltdown is the extent to which a child loses control. During a meltdown, a person with autism is completely unaware of their actions and what's happening around them. Their behavior is an involuntary, knee-jerk response to sensory overwhelm. It's almost as if they've had a complete break with reality. While it is heart-wrenching to see your child experience this, with enough awareness

and proactive intervention you can prevent them from causing harm to themselves and others.

What's the difference between a meltdown and a tantrum?

A good place to start is by understanding the difference between a sensory meltdown and a tantrum. The two are easily confused which is why many dismiss meltdowns as nothing more than a badly-behaved child's cry for attention. This couldn't be further from the truth.

Tantrums are behavioral outbursts which are a deliberate attempt to get something. A child could have a tantrum from many different reasons. They could, for example, want their parent's attention or perhaps they want their parents to buy a specific toy. Unlike meltdowns, a child having a tantrum is in control of their behavior and will most likely stop acting out when they get what they want. Tantrums and meltdown are very different and cannot be handled in the same way. By simply dismissing a meltdown as a petulant child acting out, you can cause severe harm to a child with special needs. We put together some tips which may help you calm your special child during these trying times. But remember, what calms one child with special needs may not work for another. The important thing is be understanding, patient and loving. That is after all what a child needs most during a sensory meltdown.

1. Identify and remove sensory triggers

You've probably already identified stimuli which tend to trigger meltdowns for your child. For some children with special needs this can be a visit to the town pool or a ride on a crowded bus to camp. The important thing is to be aware of your child's sensory sensitivities so you'll be prepared to act should a meltdown occur. In addition, you'll want to keep record of stimuli which make a meltdown worse. This could include loud noises or flashing lights. You may even find that talking to your child during a meltdown can exacerbate the symptoms.

2. Try distracting your child

This will only work if you spot the tell-tale signs of a meltdown before your child loses complete control. You can distract your child by doing anything which makes your child happy. The aim is to focus on something which is comforting but not over-stimulating. This could include something like making silly faces or singing your child's favorite song.

3. Make your child feel safe

Your first priority during a meltdown is to remove any triggers. This may require you to switch off music or perhaps leave a store in search of a quieter, more soothing environment. You want to do everything you can to create a quiet, cozy space where your child will feel safe. One way to do this is to put up a tent somewhere quiet. While this will help your child calm down, it isn't always an option. For those times when you can't find a quiet place to soothe your child, you can simply cradle your child in your arms until they calm down. This may take time, but it should help keep them calm.

4. Remove any dangerous objects

It's important that you remove any objects from the vicinity which could harm your child. This includes everything from glass shelves to hard objects which your child may throw. It's best to take your child to a room or space free of clutter and other people. However, it's not enough to simply isolate your child. To prevent injury during a meltdown, you'll need to monitor your child closely until they've calmed down completely.

5. Invest in a good weighted blanket
Weighted blankets are a must-have for children who have frequent meltdowns. These blankets apply mild pressure to the body, helping an anxious child calm down. In addition, the weights in the blankets help improve a child's body awareness which can reduce the severity of the meltdown. Alternatively, weighted vests give similar calming sensory feedback, and are a great option for summer and travel.

6. Always carry a pair of noise-cancelling headphones
For children who struggle with auditory stimuli, a pair of noise-cancelling headphones are a life-saver. They help reduce sensory overwhelm and can prevent the meltdown from getting out of hand.

7. Put together an emergency meltdown kit
Having an emergency kit can come in handy especially if your child tends to have meltdowns in public places. A well-stocked kit can help you defuse the situation and can make it easier to calm your child. Be sure to take this kit with you wherever you go so you'll never be caught off guard. Ideally you

should tailor the kit to suit your child's preferences. You can include things like your child's favorite toy, a body sock, a heating pad, a handheld massage ball and some aromatherapy oils.

8. Stay calm

It's essential that you try to remain as calm as possible when your child has a meltdown. Any sudden movements or aggressive actions could be perceived as a threat by your child, triggering violent behavior. It's best to talk in a soft, calm voice and to move as slowly as possible. Also, avoid any forceful behavior such as throwing your child to the ground.

9. Watch what your child eats

Food can be a potent trigger for children with sensory processing issues. Some parents resort to a gluten-free diet as they find this keeps their child calmer. If this seems too extreme, try limiting how much sugar you allow your child to consume. Carbohydrates and sugars tend to increase anxiety and anxiousness in children with autism spectrum disorder.

10. Never act without explaining

To prevent a meltdown from escalating, you need to keep your child as calm as possible. One of the best ways of doing this is by explaining what you're going to do to your child before you do it. For example, you'd say something like: *I want you to hold my hand for your safety.* Regardless of whether your child is responsive, a calm explanation can help prevent any impulse reactions.

What strategies do you have for managing and de-escalating meltdowns? Share your tips and suggestions in the comments below.

An Autistic Shutdown

Autistics have shutdowns. It's part of life. There are multiple root causes for a shutdown, including the result of sensory overload, physical and mental exhaustion, unexpected news, anxiety about an upcoming event, and upheaval in our schedule. Sometimes it comes in combination; other times it comes down to simply being "on" for so long, that we have no choice but to turn "off." Co-occurring stressors, such as physical pain, heightened anxiety, depression, post-traumatic stress, and the like, serve to further drain our energy reserves.

The amount of energy it takes a typical, non-autistic person to get through the day is, in most cases, significantly less, in comparison to an autistic's. In example, I make one hundred conscious decisions, at minimum, within the first hour of waking up. What most individuals decide subconsciously, on a type of automatic mode, I do not. The way I process life can be compared to the sensation one feels when they concentrate on their eyes blinking. When focusing on the eyes closing, we are distracted by an automatic

action that would normally not be a distraction.
Blinking doesn't involve thoughts. The way I process
is similar to the sensation of paying attention to the
blink of one's eyes: I am pulled into the blinking of my
own thoughts.

My brain, like all autistics' brains, seeks connections
through patterns. It is on super drive all day long. It
solves, reasons, rearranges, deciphers, and concludes.
Every move I make is an effort, an action I am
noticing, and behind that action multiple scaffolding
thoughts. Where in an average person might think
about six things in relation to a feasible outcome, I am
thinking of sixty. What one throws out as a die with six
sides, I throw out as ten dice with six sides. What
commonly goes unnoticed by others, is a heavy blink
to me with multiple facets, some hidden, some upright,
some tossed off the table.

The questions of how many steps to take, which room
to enter first, which task to accomplish next, which
word choice to use, how long to linger on one topic,
are not just familiarities, they are essential elements of
my existence. And behind those questions, evidence
gathered in the past, visual flashes of what has been
and what could be. In many moments, I am a bystander
set within a machine, carried where it leads, with no
steering wheel or access to controls—an entity within a
larger calculating entity. And this entity is deciphering

the feasible best route to everything, including my thinking process.

As my mind works, nothing is disqualified from being factored into an outcome. Even my toothpaste brand, how much paste I squeeze out, and the flow of the water from the faucet, are scoped out and theorized, and then neatly tucked into a web of accumulated data. My thoughts gathered, moulded, and placed into a previously opened drawer, a unit only to be reopened and reassembled during a later point of time. I am essentially a vast storage house with feelings.

Seeing as I am constantly moving within strings of webbed-data, in order to gain relief, I am instinctually drawn to a semblance of predictable patterns— something to alleviate the constant sensation of gathering, sorting, and storing.
The FAMILIAR doesn't need to be analysed. And in that there is ultimate refuge. Familiarity can come in multiple shapes and sizes—in a predictable routine, a familiar voice or face, a soothing melody, a favourite movie or book, a pattern of speech.

When I am unable to find predictable retreat in the familiarity, or when something pulls me into overload, especially when I am already at full capacity of input, I cannot help but to go into shutdown. It is automatic. My brain understands no other way to refuel and get back to a place of semi-peace. Unfortunately, the space of shutdown is not always comfortable; sometimes, it is a necessity to get me from one place to the next, like a tattered bridge, booby-trapped in a war zone, strung across and over a deep chasm of unknown.

In example, during my shutdown:

- I am unaware that I am in shutdown at the starting stage. Usually a part of me knows, but the most of me feels confused and off-balance. At this point I can do nothing but be. I have not an ounce of energy or thought process left to help myself or anyone else. I am literally a computer unplugged. **(non-responsive, unaware of surroundings, lost somewhere)**

- I might be unable to form complete thoughts or talk aloud.

- I spend the majority of time alone, in isolation and away from people. However, I could be sitting in the same room as someone else but be lost in my mind.

- I finally feel like I can breathe and not think.

- I curl up into a ball and sleep.

Shutdown leading into implosion or minor-meltdown:

- Sometimes after a shutdown (or before a shutdown), I experience an implosion of thoughts. My brain, doing what it does best, stemming out in web-like connections trying to solve a problem; only it's a problem that I cannot readily identify.

- During implosion, I turn my anger inward and use all-or-nothing self-talk. I use words like NEVER, WHAT WAS I THINKING, I CAN'T STAND THIS, I WON'T EVER DO THIS, I AM DONE WITH THAT.

- My mind, in its search for relief, makes big plans. I convince myself in the finality of my situation. That I am at last leaving something behind, turning over a new leaf, making a life altering decision. This usually means wanting to demolish an aspect of self and the way I do things. I long to become tougher, become stronger, even if that goes against my core values. I believe if I am tainted, angry, rude, better than, then I will be able to make a stand for myself.

- In implosion, I turn my back on a large part of self, thinking who I am, who I was, ultimately continually betrays me. My self-expectations are extreme. I pressure myself into rearranging aspects of self that aren't ideal. I analyze my frailties and shortcomings, both real and imagined.

- I visualize extreme decision making: I am never going on Facebook again; I am never reading about autism again; I am never going to ask him for help again; I incorporate the word AGAIN into self-talk, as a means of self-punishing myself for past decisions and actions. I criticize my past behaviors: I cannot believe I ever thought that way or acted that way; I shouldn't be this way: What is wrong with me?

- I over-exaggerate the dire state of current relationships and self-blame. Everything is ultimately somehow my fault. After all, I should have known better. What is wrong with me to think they ever cared, to have ever trusted, to have ever believed? I wallow in self-pity and hate myself for wallowing in self-pity and being trapped in the isolation chamber AGAIN.

Fortunately, part of my brain's grand analysis scheme has led me to directly dissecting my previous shutdowns and meltdowns. Given the ability to analyse elements of my experiences, I have been granted opportunity to establish certain blinking-light reminders to guide me —reminders that enable me to, at opportune moments, logically steer myself into a direction of less self-injury and poor decision-making.

It's a delicate balance, in helping self during stages of shutdown (or meltdown), as I need to allow myself not to think too heavily (in order to not fully drain all my energy reserves), but at the same time, I must allow myself opportunity to engage in some constructive self-talk. Also, there is only a finite point of time in which I will actually recognize I am in shutdown and be willing to listen to reason. Some of what I tell myself, includes:

- This has happened before; this is nothing new;

- This is part of the way your brain works;

- You will come out of this soon; you will be okay;

- Try not to follow through on any major decisions while in this state;

- You cannot reason yourself out of this, so just go with the flow;

- If you shame yourself, it's okay; it's only temporary.

As an aside, where the mental health professional veers off course, is in their thinking that traditional means of cognitive behavioural therapy will work in such shutdown mode or meltdown mode. They usually don't understand or comprehend how the mind works of an autistic, unless autistic or well versed in the matter. A counsellor implementing a set of rules in hopes of supporting a client, may indeed serve to further drown an already overburdened mind. It is a delicate dance, in which first the one in need must recognize they are trapped in the shutdown, and then maneuverer through it without over burdening the mind and causing the act of further sinking into mental exhaustion. This is difficult to explain to anyone, unless they thoroughly analyse what happens in the thinking patterns of the autistic brain.

Like everything else in an autistic world, nothing is simple, nor can be simplified.

Ask parents of kids with learning and behavioral disorders if their children experience problems with sensory processing, and many of them will answer with a resounding "yes". While it is widely accepted that most children with Autism Spectrum Disorders have trouble integrating sensory input, the fact that children who aren't on the spectrum also experience these issues to varying degrees is now being examined more closely by the special needs community. While all children can seem quirky or particular about their likes and dislikes, children with Sensory Processing Disorder (also called Sensory Integration Dysfunction) will be so severely affected by their sensory preferences that it interferes with their normal, everyday functioning. Sensory issues are usually defined as either hypersensitivity (over-responsiveness) or hyposensitivity (under-responsiveness) to sensory stimuli. Below, find some common signs of Sensory Processing Disorder.

Hypersensitivities to sensory input may include:

- Extreme response to or fear of sudden, high-pitched, loud, or metallic noises like flushing toilets, clanking silverware, or other noises that seem unoffensive to others

- May notice and/or be distracted by background noises that others don't seem to hear

- Fearful of surprise touch, avoids hugs and cuddling even with familiar adults

- Seems fearful of crowds or avoids standing in close proximity to others

- Doesn't enjoy a game of tag and/or is overly fearful of swings and playground equipment

- Extremely fearful of climbing or falling, even when there is no real danger i.e. doesn't like his or her feet to be off the ground

- Has poor balance, may fall often

Hyposensitivities to sensory input may include:

- A constant need to touch people or textures, even when it's inappropriate to do so

- Doesn't understand personal space even when same-age peers are old enough to understand it

- Clumsy and uncoordinated movements

- An extremely high tolerance for or indifference to pain

- Often harms other children and/or pets when playing, i.e. doesn't understand his or her own strength

- May be very fidgety and unable to sit still, enjoys movement-based play like spinning, jumping, etc.

- Seems to be a "thrill seeker" and can be dangerous at times

SPD and Autism

Children whose Sensory Processing Disorder conforms to the under-responsivity subtype typically require a great deal of stimulation in order to become alert and active, a behavior often seen in children with autistic spectrum disorders. Meanwhile, other children with ASD have symptoms more similar to the over-responsive subtype of SPD. Because Autism and SPD both have over-responding and under-responding categories, Autims and SPD are sometimes mistaken for one another.

The relationship between SPD and Autism is an area of great interest to scientists and families living with the condition. **Studies** by the STAR Institute suggest that at least three-quarters of children with autistic spectrum disorders have significant symptoms of Sensory Processing Disorder, and probably more depending on how significant symptoms are defined.

HOWEVER, THE REVERSE IS NOT TRUE. **Most children with SPD do not have an autistic spectrum disorder!** Our research suggests that the two conditions are distinct disorders just as SPD and ADHD are different disorders.

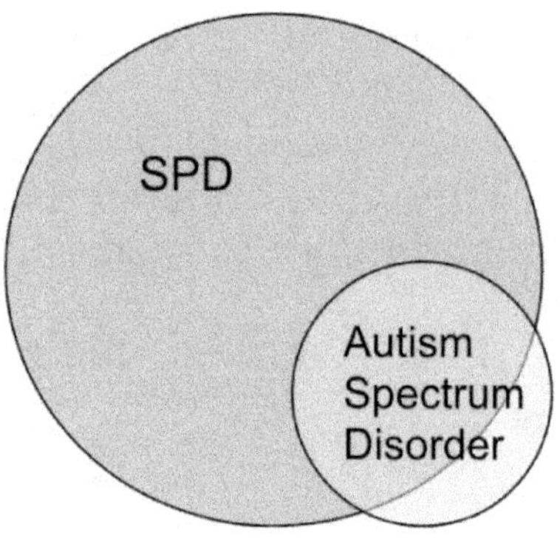

Baranek, et al, 2006,
Tomchek & Dunn 2007,
Schoen, et al 2009

Appropriate intervention relies upon accurate diagnosis. Pursuing an evaluation for SPD by a qualified occupational therapist with sensory integration training facilitates diagnosis that distinguishes autistic spectrum issues from sensory issues. This distinction increases the likelihood that your child will receive the appropriate treatment for his or her neurological conditions.

With further research into the relationship of SPD and autistic spectrum disorders, the STAR Institute hopes to facilitate better more appropriate intervention for all children who have either – or both – SPD and Autism.

SPD and ADHD

Scientists and parents alike are keenly interested in understanding the relationship between SPD and Attention Deficit Disorder (ADHD), a better-known condition that is frequently treated with medication. Although the neurological basis of the two disorders is different, children with the sensory craving subtype of SPD are especially likely to be diagnosed and treated for ADHD because their behaviors are similar to behaviors in children with Attention Deficit Disorder.

Studies by STAR Institute suggest that SPD and ADHD are unique disorders, each with its own distinct symptoms. This means that SPD is not simply a type of ADHD, and ADHD is not simply a subtype of SPD. However, an estimated 40% in the typical population and 60% in clinical samples of the children with one disorder also have symptoms of the other (**Ahn et al, 2004**).

Appropriate intervention for any disorder relies upon accurate diagnosis. Pursuing a sensory evaluation by a qualified occupational therapist with advanced training in sensory integration training facilitates diagnosis that distinguishes attention deficit issues from sensory issues. This distinction increases the likelihood that your child will receive the appropriate treatment for his or her neurological conditions. **Search the SPD Treatment Directory** to locate an OT near you.

With further research into the relationship of SPD and ADHD, the STAR Institute hopes to lay a science-based foundation for more precise diagnosis of both disorders, paving the way for better invention for all children with either one.

SPD and Misophonia

There is a significant over-lap in symptoms in what is now called "Misophonia" and SPD Sensory Over-Responsivity (SOR). Misophonia describes a neurologically based disorder in which auditory stimuli (and sometimes visual) is misinterpreted within the central nervous system. Individuals with misophonia are set off or "triggered" by very specific patterned sounds, such as chewing, coughing, pencil tapping, sneezing etc. Pawel and Jastreboff termed the disorder in 2001, in an effort to distinguish it from hyperacusis.

Hyperacusis and Misophonia are both disorders related to "decreased sound tolerance." However, hyperacusis is a condition in which auditory information is unbearably loud. In Misophonia, it is repeating (or patterned sounds) that are intolerable. The Jastreboff's (2001) originally hypothesized that in Misophonia pattern-based noises trigger an over reaction in the limbic system (where emotions are mediated in the brain). Therefore, auditory stimuli leads to an emotional response that causes the sufferer to feel anger, fear, disgust, or a generally "out of control." While the Jastreboff's distinguished between hyperacusis and misophonia via their symptoms, the confusion between the two disorders is far from resolved. The etiology of both disorders is also not clear.

SPD SOR and Misophonia share a remarkable symptom overlap. In both Misophonia and Sensory Over-Responsivity auditory stimuli sets off fight/flight, leaving the sufferer feeling angry, fearful, disgusted and/or "generally out of control" as the Jastreboff's originally suggested.

The research in Misophonia is in its infancy. However, an impressive body of research in Sensory Over-Responsivity has emerged over the last 15 years. The work in Sensory Over-Responsivity includes numerous physiologic studies demonstrating that upon presentation of sensory stimuli children and adults are propelled into the fight/flight response. Due to the symptom overlap, it is important that misophonia researchers collaborate with SPD researchers in an effort to understand the similarities and differences between the disorders and also to inform the misophonia research in general.

Sensory Processing Disorder, also known as SPD, is a condition in which the brain struggles to properly respond to information taken in by the senses. Often, this results in people with the disorder being overly sensitive to things in their environment. Normal sounds and textures can be painful or overwhelming to those with SPD. For example, merely touching a shirt or a piece of velvet can trigger this pain. As a result, people with SPD may be uncoordinated, hard to converse with, or even unable to tell where their limbs are in space.

Typically, sensory processing issues are identified in children, although adults can have them as well. Sensory Processing Disorder is frequently seen in children who have other conditions like autism spectrum disorder. Much like autism spectrum, the symptoms of this disorder exist on a spectrum. However, unlike autism, it is possible for the child to outgrow this disorder. Let's examine the different possible cases for someone with SPD.

In the less severe cases, a child may just have an immature sensory system. Thus, he or she will be able to outgrow it as they develop and their sensory system matures. However, sometimes the disorder is permanent, and the child must learn to develop coping strategies. Such strategies can include social withdrawal, or other, healthier things like swimming to reduce this stress.

Unfortunately, Sensory Processing Disorder is not being fully researched and recognized by the health care community. Many feel that there is no real hardcore evidence of this disorder. Thus, without concrete evidence it can be difficult to study and quantify the symptoms and causes of SPD. However, there have been some studies done, that found similarities between ADHD and SPD. A child with SPD often faces similar symptoms as one with AHDD — restless, easily distracted, impulsive, forgetful, and more. However, symptoms like a desire to swing or spin and a fear of walking on grass are unique to SPD.

Although SPD share similarities with ADHD, the traditional ADHD medications do not work on those with SPD. Rather, a child with SPD needs to work with an occupational therapist to reduce or remove their symptoms. Treatment ranges from swinging on a trapeze to touching Play Doh, all activities that stimulate the senses. After around a month of such treatment, most children will start to feel more comfortable and even physically stronger. For some, this treatment needs to last for years in order to show progress. Overall, it is possible to remedy or outgrow SPD, although it is a case by case situation.

Poor **sensory processing** can affect all developmental domains (cognitive, social emotional, motor, speech and language, and adaptive). There are **three** main **patterns of sensory processing problems** that you may see in the **children** you care for: over-responsiveness, under-responsiveness, and **sensory** seeking.

For many parents, learning that sensory processing issues are the root of some of their child's behaviors can provide relief. But it can also raise a lot of questions—specifically, "What can I do to help?" Here are some steps to help you get started.

1
Learn all you can about sensory processing issues.

There's a lot to know **about sensory processing issues**. Become familiar with **terms** your child's teachers, doctors and specialists might use. Understand what sensory processing issues can **look like at different ages** and how **signs can change over time**. And debunk **common myths**.

2
Observe your child's sensory triggers.

There are **common triggers for kids with sensory processing issues**. But no two children with sensory processing issues are affected in exactly the same way.

Sensory processing issues can cause struggles with taste, touch, noise, smells, visual stimulation, or a combination of these. They can also **affect motor skills**. Some kids may be undersensitive while others are oversensitive—and some may experience both. **Observe your child and take notes**. This can help you identify her unique trouble spots and find solutions.

3

Look into treatments and strategies for sensory processing issues.

An **occupational therapist** can design a "**sensory diet**" routine for your child. This is a type of **sensory integration** intervention or treatment strategy for kids with sensory processing issues. A sensory diet can help your child get into a "just right state" to make it easier for her to learn and pay attention. It can include a series of physical activities for your child to do. It may also include accommodations like **fidget toys**.

4

Discuss supports and services for sensory processing issues with the school.

Even if the school has done its own evaluation, **recommendations from outside evaluations** can help **determine if your child is eligible** for an IEP or a 504 plan. With an IEP or a 504 plan, your child would be able to get formal accommodations. If she's not eligible, learn about **informal supports** that could help.

You can also request that the school do a sensory profile test. This can help teachers identify how sensory processing issues affect your child during the school day—and **how to help**. If your child's school has not been involved in identifying her sensory processing issues, schedule a meeting with the school and provide a copy of the report from the specialist or pediatrician.

5

Get tips for managing meltdowns.

Kids with sensory processing issues often struggle with self-regulation. They can have intense reactions—reactions that can be hard for parents to understand and know how to manage.

Learn about **the difference between a tantrum and a sensory meltdown**. Some parents and professionals may use the terms interchangeably, but they're different behaviors. Compare the **signs of each** and **helpful ways to handle them**.

6

Understand the possible emotional impact.

Having learning and attention issues can also have an effect on your child's emotions. In some cases, there's even a higher risk for mental health issues. Learn about the **signs of anxiety and depression**. Don't wait to contact your child's doctor if you have any concerns.

7

Discover ways to help with sensory processing issues at home.

Creating and sticking to routines can be especially helpful for kids with sensory processing issues. But so can being **flexible around your child's clothing choices** and finding ways to accommodate for the things she's sensitive to. Explore a collection of tips to **help kids with sensory processing issues at home**.

If your child is undersensitive to painful stimuli, you may be worried about her safety. It's important to have specific discussions about this with your child. For example: "If you fall down or see blood, tell a grown-up right away." If you need to loop in friends and family for help, get tips on **how to explain sensory processing issues** to them.

8

Find support.

Contact your local **Parent Training and Information Center** (PTI) to learn about local services that can help. Search online for sensory-friendly events near you, like **sensory-friendly movies**. Read about other parents' experiences with sensory processing issues, like how one family **created a sensory-friendly Halloween**or a mom's **approach to coping with her child's sensory challenges**.

And be sure to connect with other parents of children with sensory processing issues in our **online community**.

9

Stay in touch with the school.

Continue to **talk with the teacher about how sensory processing issues affect your child**. Share coping strategies that work for your child. Then use that information to find ways to make potentially tricky school situations, like **field trips**, go more smoothly.

This is going to be about the hypersensitivity of the

senses.

Sound: my hearing is so good that I can hear my own hart beat, my own breaths, my head pounding, ear whiling, skin tubing, cloths rubbing, my own swallowing, teeth chattering, everything from my body I can hear in 10x volume.

I can hear every sound my house makes. the hum of the lights, the buzz of the TV, the hum of the fans, the creaks of the wood expanding and contracting, the tick tock of a clock, the grind of a computer hard drive, the fly flying around in the other end of the house. I hear everting in 10x mode. I can hear the buzz a TV makes when it is on but no sound is coming out of it and I can hear it from the other end of the house.

I can hear every car moving from miles around and can detect different engine sounds from each and every one of them. I can hear car doors opening and closing from miles around. I can hear people talking from miles around and sometimes if I concentrate I can make out what they are saying and repeat it back to anyone listening to me.

I can hear every plane flying within miles of me and can pick out the different sounds different plans make or whether it is a helicopter instead. I can hear every ferry that passes by and can tell how fast they are going based on the sound that they make. all of this at 10x volume.

when I go into a crowded space with lots of people talking, I can hear every conversation all at once and it just gets overwhelming.

No wonder why I like it alone by myself in a secluded space where there is very few sounds to deal with. NO wonder why I hate eating out or going to the movies or anywhere where there is lots of people. I hear everything at 10x so it is an amazing thing if I can respond to people under theses situations.

This is just me, but it may be your kids to

 that have it just as bad as I do. Keep that in-

mind the next time they have a melt down in

public. they just have not learned to adapt to

the mass amount of information their brains are trying

to deal with.

Smell: my smell is so good that I can detect the

smallest amounts of smell off of people, animals, food,

drink ext. I can not stand perfume or cologne because

there is too much smell to deal with. I smell things

with 10x the smell senses then a NT person does.

I can smell the mill that is two towns over with its Sulphur scented smoke pouring in the air. the higher the concentration of the smell the more chance of rain that we will have in my town.

I can smell the grass from inside my house with all the windows closed. I can smell the trees and flowers the same way. I always keep my windows and doors closed to not have to smell as strongly the outside smells.

I can just walk by someone and know if they are wearing perfume or cologne or even deodorant that day.

some smells I like so I want to smell more of them others I hate and gag if I even start to smell them.

I can smell other peoples cooking from 4 doors down and can tell what they are having for supper.

smell is a funny thing because it does not affect me nearly as much as some of the senses it is a minor inconvenience to me but does not hurt me.

TOUCH: I feel everything at 10x strength. I feel every imperfection in my clothes, and it bugs me to no end sometimes.

I can feel every little ting going on in my body. I feel my hart pumping, my chest rising and falling, my lungs filling and emptying of air, my ribs moving up and down, the pain in my ribs with each movement, the pain in my chest as this movement happens, the pain in my finger joints trying to type this out, the hart palpitations with working on this blog, the throb of blood running through my body and brain, the throb of the blood in my ear, the pain in both my elbows, the bad pain in my back and neck, the pain in my toe joints and the balls of my feet that ache all the time, the hip pain that is giving me a limp, the bad headache that I always seem to have.

I feel everything that touches my body or that I touch with my body by 10x.

When I shake your hand it hurts me to do it but I do it because it is what is expected of me.

when I knock on a door it also hurts me and I do it for the same reasons.

wearing cloths put me in constant pain that I have just gotten used to and live with it.

I do not like wearing glasses, but I cannot see at all without them, so I put up with them, but they hurt me a lot.

I wear shoes so my feet don't get wet, but they really hurt me and cause lots of pain for me.

I wear a hat to keep my head dry and my eyes shielded

but it itches my head and hurts my head and I would

rather not wear it, but it is better then the other way.

It hurts me when people touch any part of me, I really

hate people touching my hair or shoulder it is painful

and hurtful and i do not like it.

It hurts me every time i have to make a step but if I do

not, I will not go anywhere so I trudge through the pain

and hurtfulness and take those steps.

blankets touching me can cause me pain and

discomfort and so can pillows and sheets.

99% of the pain and hurt I feel is caused by me

experiencing way too much felling with touch.

I wish I found not feel anything it would have

to be better then what it is for me because I

can not last much longer with all the hurt and pain, I have to deal with each and every day just to get up out of bed is painful and hurtful for me.

SIGHT: I have had more problems with sight then any other except touch. I had a lazy eye when I was a kid and had to have it patched for months to fix it. I have 400/20 vision in my left and 200/20 vision in my right.

I have no depth perception or spacial awareness of any kind. I can not see any motion of any kind either so most sports are out.

My vision is always blurry even with glasses they are blurry and staticky looking. I have very poor night vision if at all.

I bump into stuff all the time and it hurts. I stub my toes on stuff all the time and they really hurt. I trip over my feet all the time and it hurts and throes me off balance and makes me fall down a lot of the time.

I have a hard time telling what is real and what is not real because my vision is so bad, I cannot see enough detail to tell for sure.

I see blotches of shapes that fade in and out of my vision that distract me and make it hard to concentrate.

I have a hard time reading because all the words get jumbled together for me and I have to say each one in my head slowly for me to be able to read it properly. I am a slow reader, but I do get more out of what I read then some people do.

I cannot read stuff when I am moving to and from them the words just go out of focus and can not be read.

I cannot read time if it is not in a stable point for the

same reason. that is why I wear a watch or that I always have the time close at hand.

I cannot see my body if I am in motion. if my arms or legs are in motion, I cannot see them they are just a blur going by and not distingisble.

I have to look at my feet and try to predict where they are going to land and adjust on the fly for them to land on a flat and stable spot so that I don't fall down.

I have to be careful of ware my hands and arms are at all times so that they do not accidentally hit, smack or otherwise get into trouble that I did not mean for them to get into.

I also have to do the same for my legs and feet because it can happen so fast that there is nothing I can do to stop it once it has begun.

I see 10x lighter then there really is so I prefer to do

work in a dusky semi dark room with little light and

windows with blinds turned tight. right now, I am in

such a room typing this up for you. no lights on just a

little light coming through the blind slits.

I see even less without my glasses but even with them

I do not really see much at all.

I hate having my fair washed, brushed or cut because it

hurts me and I am afraid of the water, hair brush, and

clippers.

I shield my eyes from the sun and other bright lights

because they hurt my eyes and are painful to look at.

I have selective hearing and difficulty hearing because

there is too much sounds going on around me and I can

not filter or focus on

just one or two sounds I hear them all and my Brian

tries to focus on them all. which means i may not hear you or have trouble understanding you.

I am a picky eater: I resist new foods and textures. I taste, smell and feel everything that goes in my mouth. It takes me a long time to get used to a certain taste, feel, smell of foods so I do not like to change them because I like to know what I am going to experience when I eat something.

I complain about tags in my clothing because they scratch my back and make it itchy and they hurt me and overwhelm my sense of touch.

I seem to be unaware of normal touch or pain: I often touch others too soft or too hard. I can not tell how hard or soft I am touching someone. a firm hand shake could really hurt the other person. I tend to feel way more pain then normal from myself, but I can not tell if

I am causing pain to others.

I hate being tickled or cuddled. Tickling overwhelms me and hurt me. cuddling overwhelms me and has to be done in a very slow and intentional way.

I have poor gross motor skills such as running and riding a bike. I do run like a girl even worse than one, but I did learn how to ride a bike by the time I was 7 and am ok at riding bikes.

I have trouble focusing and/or concentrating. It takes me forever to get anything done because I keep losing focus on it and just pace for a while. I am a procrastinator and perfectionist so i get nothing done ever. this blog and hopefully my book with be the first things that I have ever finished.

I am overly sensitive to loud sounds such as vacuums

and blenders. I freak out when the vacuum or blender or popcorn maker is on the sounds from them hurt my ears and make me very nervous.

I am always smelling people food and objects. I smell everything around me before I have anything to do with it. it just helps me to know the smells that I will have to get used to. so that I do not freak out because of a smell that I do not recognize.

I chew on everything. well I used to chew on everything, but it has been a long time since I have done any chewing other then food. I used to like the stimuli in my mouth of chewing and sucking on anything I could get my hands on.

I have poor fine motor skills: such as handwriting and cutting. My handwriting is worse then a doctor and even I can not read it some of the time. I can not read my printing some of the time either. I can not cut to save my life I always end up going in zig zag patterns when I try to cut something I can not cut straight.

I have difficulty dressing myself. well I used to but with being a only child and my mom a stay at home mom we would spend hours taking cloths off and putting them back on. using different outfits and different styles. doing a lot of changing from my pjs to my regular cloths and back again. by the time I was 7 I could dress myself sometimes not too well, but I did get better and do a pretty good job these days.

I sit with my legs in a "W" position. I do this all the time because it hurts less then siting cross legged. do not ask me why it hurts less but it does, and it provides more stimuli if needed then cross leaded.

I put my socks on just so or maybe i never go barefoot.

I have to ware my socks just so or else it drives me made. I can not have my socks droopy it itches my legs when that happens. I have to ware socks if I ware pants because I can not stand the pants touching my ankles because of how much it itches them. I will go bare foot if I am wearing shorts.

I would much rather go naked because then there would be lots less stimuli to deal with. I just would need to get used to the cold. I only were cloths because it is what is expected of me not what I want to do myself.

This is the end of this session, but I will go into more detail about some of these areas in a latter date. also, I am going to do a lot of talking about each sense and what it is like for me to have them so hyperactive.

I have very bad low muscle tone. I can not even use my left

arm or hand because of it and my left leg is not much better.

Thank god I am right handed because I would be hooped

otherwise. I did a test with a kid that has no use of his left arm

or hand either and I made him print his name with his good

hand and bad hand and then I would do the same. I said that he

would be able to print better with his bad hand then I could

with my good and I won the bet. I could not print at all with my

bad hand. I could not get my hand to move to make a letter let

alone print my name. and his bad hand printing was more

legible then my good hand. It made him feel really good about

him self.

He was down on him self saying that his disorder was

preventing him from getting a job.

I showed him that he was no ware near as bad a I

am, and I have gotten jobs before. This was in

collage in my program for people with disabilities. I

had very prominent ears when I was little, but my

parents had them surgically altered to look normal

so that I would not get teased even more badly then

I was at school. I really wish they had not bothered

to change them I feel robed of my look that I liked. I

used to say that I had Dumbo ears because when I

bounced my ears would flop up and down. I do not

think it would have made a difference in school with

regards to the teasing and bullying. it was bad enough wearing

glasses, being clumsy, acting unusual and the such that having

Dumbo ears would not have caused any more problems for me

then I already had.

All of my joints are hyper extensible and hyper mobile. all of

them are also double jointed. the things I can do with my

fingers and toes would amaze you. As a result, I can crack all

of my joints and they tend to dislocate a lot of the time. I am

always in pain in one part of my body or another. My neck,

back, ribs, elbows, fingers, knees and toe joints are my most painful and the most often to be cracking and dislocating. I have had lots of problems with my feet hurting

dew to the flatness of them. I wear orthotics to help

with it, but they do not do a very good job. I tend to

lean back and left all the time. I know this because I have Wii

fitness and the fitness board, and it does balance tests and said

that I am not balanced that i lean left and back. I am trying to

work on that but the pain in my feet and it affects my knees and

hips also so they are always in pain also as a result of me

leaning left and back.

I have squinted and tend to turn my eyes to the side

and down all of my life that I can remember. I tend

to close my eyes when people take my picture with

the flash on because the flash hurts my eyes. my

eyelids usually are puffy, and I get bad itchy eyes

that water a lot of the time. I find there is too much

light and too much stimuli to keep my eyes open

and looking straight. I never turn lights on in the

house because I do not need them to see just fine. my vision is

connately blurry and staticky all of the time. I have just gotten

used to it and it does not bother me all the much any more.

I am considered legally blind without my glasses. I had lazy

eye when I was little and had to ware a patch for 2 months

when I was 3 to fix the lazy eye. I am very far sighted with a

400/20 vision in my left eye and 200/20 in my right eye. It was

my left eye that was lazy and still is a little lazy even today. I

can not see any motion of any kind and have no depth

perception or spacial awareness

ss. That is why sports are pretty much out of the

question because if you can not see any motion you

can not play sports with moving objects that are

coming at you. they just bounce off of you and or

fly past you, so it is not worth tying to play them. although I tried very hard to play all sports and failed miserably at all of them except golf and bowling. That is also why I choose not to drive because I can not see the sings or tell where the other cars are in relation to my car.

I have been hospitalized 19 times over the years since I was 17. the last time was a three months ago. I have had to change my meds more times than I can count. So, if you are noticing any strange behaviour or lots of bad meltdowns on meds it might be the meds causing them. You may have trouble getting any doc to think that the meds are the problem but trust me they defiantly can be. I am not saying that the meds will be the problem just that they might be.

I had a lot of trouble with speech when I was little right up till, I was 14. I had a speech doc till I was 16. I used to stutter a lot too when I would get anxious. I am for the most part pretty good these days. A lot has to do with Being a lot less anxious these days.

the only time I can ever remember getting seizures is from bad side effect from meds, but I may get them all the time and not now about it.

10 years ago, my doc put me on Omega 3

 fish oils and I had a really good improvement to them. He said that the brain

needs oils to better communicate and so the

fish oils will improve my brains ability to

communicate. I highly recommend you try it

for your ASDers because it really works. It

makes you think more clearly, remember

things better, pay more attention to stuff,

react quicker to stuff, and so much more. You should talk to your doc about the benefits that Omega 3 fish oils could have on your ASDers.

I started to get asthma like attacks starting when I was 10 and got really bad by the time, I was 13. Through testing to find out what was going wrong they found out that I have a hart murmur. They thought that that might be what was causing me to pass out from lack of oxygen to my brain. So, they put me on a hart monitor and made me do stress tests to find out what my hart was doing during my pass-outs. I would do the stress test fine and within a couple of minuets of stoping I would have a attack and pass out for a few seconds. They did not find that my hart was the problem it seemed to function properly. So, they called it exercise induced asthma. I like to call it anxiety induced asthma because I think it is more to do with my anxiety getting out of control and not breathing properly so not getting enough oxygen to my muscles and brain. My muscles get very weak and my head gets light headed after an attack. As

I get older and get my anxiety under control my attacks rarely happen any more these days.

When I was 12, I got athletes foot, jock itch, and toe fungus. I have been struggling to deal with these problems all my life since then. To this day I still have all three and they are progressively getting worse each and every year that goes by.

When I was 12, I started to get severe joint pain in my knees and elbows. I started to crack them on a hourly basics to keep the pressure and some of the pain under control. To this day I have to do this and now I where braces on my knees and elbows to help with the pain.

My doc says it is caused by low muscle tone in the joints and the tendons having to do all the work without help from the muscles.

In the last 5 years or so I have also been getting severe left hip pain because I have been leaning on my left leg to keep some of the pressure off of my right leg which is in worse shape then the left leg. It gets so bad that I can not stand or walk and can not sleep because of how bad the pain is.

For me I am allergic to grapes, bananas, corn, dairy, gluten, oranges, peanuts, MSG, and all other preservatives, plus I think there are others that I just have not found out about. I am also allergic to dust, pollen from grass and trees, weeds, flowers, I have hey-fever also. Plus, I am allergic to cats and some dogs also. My allergies are so bad that I always have trouble breathing through my nose because it is so clogged most of the time. I have a perpetual runny nose with sneezing in-between. It really gets on my nerves sometimes about how much stuff I am allergic to and how bad the reactions are to most of the stuff that I am allergic to.

Overview of Stimming in Autism

The term "stimming" is short for self-stimulatory behaviour and is sometimes also called "stereotypic" behaviour. In a person with autism, stimming usually refers to specific behaviour's that include hand- flapping, rocking, spinning, or **repetition of words and phrases**.

Stimming is almost always a **symptom of autism**, and it's usually the most obvious. After all, few typically developing people rock, flap, pace, or flick their fingers on a regular basis. While autistic stimming does look unusual, however, it's important to note that subtler forms of stimming are also a part of most people's behaviour patterns. If you've ever tapped your pencil, bitten your nails, twirled your hair, or tapped your toes, you've engaged in stimming.

The biggest differences between autistic and typical stimming are the type, quantity, and obviousness of the behaviour.

Which Behaviours Are Considered to Be Stims?

In general, behaviours are described as "stims" when they go beyond what is culturally tolerated. In other words, a "stim" is a behaviour that is culturally unacceptable.

While it's at least moderately acceptable in the United States to bite one's nails or twirl one's hair, for example, it's considered unacceptable to wander around flapping one's hands. Mild and occasional rocking is usually acceptable but rocking one's entire body back and forth is considered to be a stim.

There's really no good reason why flapping should be less acceptable than nail-biting (it's certainly more hygienic!). But in our world, the hand flappers receive negative attention while the nail-biters (at least to a certain degree) are tolerated.

Some stims can be quite extreme and are legitimately upsetting or even frightening to typical people. For example, some autistic people stim by making loud noises that can sound threatening or scary. Some hit themselves with their hands, or even bang their heads against the wall. These types of stims are obviously problematic for a variety of reasons.

When Do Autistic People Stim?

For most people, stimming occurs only now and then. People with autism, however, often find it difficult to stop stimming, and may do it during most of their waking hours.

People with autism may stim because they are excited, happy, anxious, overwhelmed, or because it feels comforting. Under stressful circumstances, they may stim for long periods of time.

Most of us are aware of and can control our stims (we wouldn't bite our nails, for example, while having a romantic dinner). If we feel the need to stim in a stressful situation, we are usually careful to be subtle about it. For example, we might tap our toes under the table rather than rock back and forth. People with autism, however, may not be aware of and responsive to others' reactions to their stims. There seem to be circumstances in which some people with autism are not able to control their stims or find it extremely stressful and difficult to do so.

Why Do Autistic People Stim?

It's not completely clear why stimming almost always goes along with autism, though most experts say that it's a tool for "self-regulation" and self-calming. As such, it may well be an outgrowth of the **sensory processing dysfunction** that often goes along with autism.

People with autism stim to help themselves to manage anxiety, fear, anger, excitement, anticipation, and other strong emotions. They also stim to help themselves handle overwhelming sensory input (too much noise, light, heat, etc.). There are also times when people stim out of habit, just as neurotypical people bite their nails, twirl their hair, or tap their feet out of habit.

At times, stimming can be useful, making it possible for the autistic person to manage challenging situations. When it becomes a distraction, creates social problems, or causes physical harm to self or others, though, it can get in the way of daily life.

Tips for Managing Stims

Should stimming behaviour be forbidden or "extinguished" through therapy? In general, unless the behaviour is dangerous, there is no reason to forbid it—but there are a number of reasons to manage it.

- Unlike most people, individuals with autism may self-stimulate constantly. As a result, stimming may stand between them and their ability to interact with others, take part in ordinary activities, or even be included in typical classrooms, community venues, or places of employment.

- Stimming can be a distraction to others and, in some cases, can actually be upsetting. A child who regularly needs to pace the floor or slap himself in the head is certain to be a distraction for typical students—and in some extreme cases, stimming can be frightening to watch.

- Stimming can draw negative attention. Autistic children and adults are often socially marginalized because of their unusual or disturbing behaviors.

Lessening or modifying stims can be tricky. Stims are a tool for managing sensory and emotional input, so simply punishing a child for stimming can cause far more harm than good. At the very least, the process should be slow and responsive to the needs of the individual.

- **Applied Behavior Analysis (ABA)**, a behavioral therapy, may help individuals to eliminate or modify some of their stimming.

- **Occupational therapists** can provide a "sensory diet" to help reduce the need for stims.

- In some cases, stimming can be reduced with **medications** that address underlying issues of anxiety.

- Environmental and social environments can be changed to make anxiety less likely. Smaller classes, quieter settings, and clearer expectations can all go a long way to lower stress.

- Finally, some people with autism can learn through practice and coaching to either change their stims (squeeze a stress ball rather than flap, for example) or engage in excessive stimming only in the privacy of their own homes.

Stimming is rarely dangerous. It can, however, be embarrassing for parents and siblings, disconcerting for teachers, or off-putting for potential friends and co-workers. To what degree should others' discomfort dictate how autistic people should behave? That's a question that must be answered by the individuals involved, including the autistic person him or herself.

While it may well be possible to reduce stimming, though, it may be impossible to eliminate it altogether. As the parent or caregiver for a person with autism, it may be necessary to simply accept the reality that your autistic family member behaves differently from his or her typical peers. This isn't always easy, especially if you're very sensitive to the judgments of others. If you need to, consider seeking professional counselling to help you manage your feelings and frustrations.

When I was 16 my parents made me go to a psychiatrist. I did not want to go but they made me, so I went. The doc sent less than a hour with me and said I had OCD and put me on 20mg of Paxil and 1mg of Anafenel to combat the symptoms.

I was also on a med for my acne which was a high dose of vitamin A.

With in a couple of weeks I was felling way better and all of my anxiety had gone away. But it

 did not last long because within another couple of weeks all hell broke louse. I started acting out and having massive meltdowns for no apparent reason. So, they upped the meds to 30mg of Paxil and 1.25mg of anafenel.

In a couple more weeks it got even worse and I started hitting and biting and flipping out.

The docs said mental illness can appear around this age and so did nothing about it. One day I skipped school took a sledge hammer to the side door and trashed the house Thorley and took everything of value out of the hose in garbage bags into the empty lot next door.

When I was done, I called 911 to report that the house had been broken into. So, the police came by and took statements. My parents got home just minutes after the police had showed up.

They were devastated at what had been done to their house.

A couple of days latter I went to look at the bags of stuff that I had took because it had snowed the day before.

My mom found my tracks and found the stash of stuff and was really exited and got me and my dad to lug the bags back to the house and check that everything was in them that was stolen and sure enough all was accounted for. They called the cops and the cops came and took fingerprints off of the bags and made us come down to the station to get our finger prints taken.

So that night I freaked out because I knew my prints would be all over those bags and got caught by my parents when I tried to steal the computer back again.

They informed the police that I had done it and not to go to all of the effort.

The police wanted me to get some help, but they never did.

the next day I was put in the psych ward at the hospital because

I had such terrible panic attacks because I had broken the only computer in the house, and I could not live without a computer to play with.

I stayed in the psych ward for almost a month till they finally said I had to leave they needed my bed.

They did lots of testing on me but all they could come up wit h was that I was social phobic with other anxiety disorders and they did not know why I was behaving the way that I was.

My dad visited me every day in the ward and we would talk and go for walks and do stuff together. My mom never came to se me not even once. My dad said she could not bare to see me like that it hurt too much and all she could do was cry.

I went home and went back to school, but I did not last more than two weeks before it got so bad that I just dropped out of school.

I stayed home by myself for four months before my parents were able to get me into a special hospital for kids with disabilities.

I had to stay their for three weeks to get a bunch of tests done on me to find out what was going on.

I was supposed to have weekend visits with my parents where I got to go home and then come back on Monday. But they decided I was not ready when the first weekend visit was supposed to happen. So, they said I could not go home for the weekend and would only be able to go out for a few hours each day.

My dad told them that I was going to make a run for it and there was nothing that they could do to stop me. they said not to worry this is a locked ward and there is no way that he can get out of here.

Well every day they have a shift change and we are sent to our rooms that are not locked and made to wait their till they come for us.

That day I did not wait I snuck out of my room there was no one around and so I wandered out the door into the hall and told the security guard that I had a pass to go for a walk and he let me outside and I made a run for the road out of their. I ran for two blocks before I had to slow down to a walk and kept on going heading for the highway to go home.

I waked for four hours before someone stopped and offered me a ride. He thought I was a friend of his, but he felt sorry for me, so he gave me a ride.

the hospital was 60 miles away from the ferry terminal that I had to take to get home. I had walked 12 miles by that point and was dead tired and had planned to sleep in the ditch till morning and continue on.

I gave him all the money I had which was $6 to pay for the gas he used to get me to the ferry. I made the last ferry home and one of the ferry workers recognized me and new my parents were in Victoria spending the weekend with me their because my dad had talked to him on his way over to town.

So, he gave me a ride home and got in touch with my dad about me being at home.

I called the hospital to tell them where I was and to tell my parents that that is where I was.

I spent the night with no one at home me all by myself and my parents came home the next day. they got home in the early afternoon, so I had the whole house to myself. I liked it that way and I did not mind it one bit and got into no trouble at all. We spent the weekend talking and trying to figure things out and went home Monday morning back to the hospital to finish with the testing.

They clanged my med to 10mg of Paxil and 1mg of risperidone. It did not help me much, but they had to try something. With in a day of the change I threatened to burn the place to the ground and that I saw flames erupting from every ware.

All they could say is that I have PDD-NOS but could not tell us anything useful.

We got home and the psychiatrist changed the meds again to 50mg of Zoloft and 1.25mg of risperidone.

Things went from bad to worse within a couple of weeks I had set the house on fire and was a ranting lunatic.

The cops charged me with arson and sent me for a psych eval at a youth detention facility.

Their they took me off all my meds because they could not get them to me.

I spent a month in their and they came back that I was a hypochondriac and there was nothing wrong with me at all.

The courts put me on house arrest till they figured out what to do with me.

My parents got a good lawyer to fight the case and it took 8 months to get it all figured out.

Eventually the case was dropped with it being labelled mental incompetency to stand trail.

So, After the prison I went home, and my parents did not know what to do with me because the hose was toast and they were living in a tent while it was being repaired.

So, they got me back into that hospital that I was talking about for more tests.

I went their for 5 weeks because I was so much better off of all

the meds that they did not know what to say to my parents. they

wanted

 to say that I needed to be put in a nut house and never let out.

But I was so much better that that was no longer a option.

After all the tests they came back with Asperger's Syndrome as

the DX for me.

I got to go home with my parents and they still did not know

what to do with me, so they put me into a full time youth care

home.

Their I lived and was only allowed to see my parents every

second week.

i hated it their and it was not a good experience for me.

I lived their for over a year till finally I had to leave because I

had gotten too old for them. I had turned 19 and was out of the

youth system and into the adult one.

The insurance company did not want to pay the claim on the

fire damage to the house. But eventually once the court

dropped the charges, they decided they had to pay up and so

they paid my parents $90000 for the repairs that needed to be done on the house.

I went into a day program for persons with disabilities for the next 8 months and really enjoyed it as I got to work on a ranch taking care of horses. I got to ride the horses too which I liked about it also.

After that I got into a vocational program at the local collage that was a two-year course and I did really well in it.

After that I went and got my Computer Service Technician Diploma and have never looked back since.

I am doing a lot better but still have some issues to work out. I have to be very carful what I take including herbal stuff as it can cause a similar reaction with me. 9 years ago, I ended up fired from my job and arrested for steeling and ended up in the hospital psych ward because of an herbal supplement for allergy relief. I did get my job back after 6 months but was not allowed to handle cash. I have since stopped working there and now work at the library putting books away.

I have a real problem keeping warm I am always freezing and

unless it is really warm out, I will still be wearing a sweater. I

rarely sweat unless it is really hat out. I joke to my parents that

I am cold blooded because it is so hard for me to keep warm.

When I do get hot it is hard for me to cool down but that is a

very rare occasion. I think it does mess with the internal

temperatures. I have heard from others that they are usually

over hot. I can not stay in the pool for more than 20min before my teeth

start to chatter. I also have the problem of getting sun-stroked very easily

too.

I do a lot of typical autism stimming. I hand flap

when I am very excited. I rock, pace, spin, I stare at

fans when they are on for the spinning of the

blades. I rock when I am upset. I pace when I have

to release some frustrations but sometimes I just

pace to be able to think. I do not know why I spin, but I like it a lot. When I am around other people with autism that are stimming, I tend to stim more mimicking their stemming. That is why I try not to get too close to others while they are stimming because I do not want people to see me stimming. I am embarrassed that I do it. I do not mean to do it it just happens, and I sometimes do not like that I do it but I can not control myself.

I have a congested nose almost all year long and

unless it is a runny and sneezy nose Claritin will not

help it. I do not know what would help maybe

Breath-right strips to help open up the nostrils. I do not know

what causes it but I do find it to hurt my sleeping at times.

I get really anxious if I stim in public, I do not want people to

see me as disabled but I have found I get treated better when people know

that I am disabled then if they don't. The only jobs that I have ever gotten

was ones where I told them that I was disabled.

I struggled with poty training till I was 13 years old. I was good at home but struggled away from home especially at school. I did not like using public washrooms I did not know who else had used them and what they had done in them.

I just could not get up the nerve to ask to go to the washroom at school and that had dire consequences.

I am on 10 mg of olanzapine for anti-psychotic, 0.5 mg of clonazepam for anxiety, 10 mg abilify for my behaviors, 500 mg divalproex for my mood swings, 900 mg omega 3 fish oils for brain health, and 2000 iu vitamin d because I do not go outside much.

Yes, I do have crazy ups and downs that I can not figure out what causes them or how to get out of them. they used to last for months but now they last for a couple of weeks and then stop. You go through depression cycles all the time. The divalproex helps a lot with the crazy mood swings.

You have to be very careful when using meds and if the

behaviors get worse then wean them off and try another, but I

have found that the right mix of meds can make all the world of

difference. and just because my mix works for me does not

mean it would work in your case.

I started to get severe weakness in my legs, loss of stamina and

decreased ability for fitness. Plus, shortness of breath and really

feeling weak after doing any amount of physical activity. this

for me started by age 11 and as gotten progressively worse over

the years. I used to be good at track and field 100 m and 400 m

races but had to stop doing them by the time I was 12 because

of how bad it had gotten. I used to play lots of sports but now I

can only play golf and bowling and even those are difficult for

me especially the golf. I just don't have the stamina to do more

than 9 holes. The docs said it was exercised induced asthma,

but I do not think that is it at all.

I have a hart murmur that causes a very irregular

hart beat. I can notice my hart stop beating for

several seconds then start up again. and it is all

over the place with the beats. I think that is why I

can not do physical activity because my hart can not pump the

blood in a way that gets the oxygen to the muscles fast enough.

In February of 2010 I started a herbal drug for allergies

called quesertan. My mom thought it would be better

than Claritin because it was herbal. It had dire

consciences and made this really bad for me. I started

hallucinating and hearing voices. I started stealing

money and goods from home and work. I started acting

out and lying to everyone. it went on like this till April.

My parents decided to leave me at home for two weeks

by myself while they went to palm springs to go

golfing. On April 21st of 2010 I was arrested for theft

and escorted to the back office where we waited for the

police. they asked me questions and I told them I have

autism and that the voices told me to do it which was true to both accounts. the police came and handcuffed me and hulled out of the store into a police car where I was read my rights and what I was charged with and let go. I was in total melt down mode and did not know what to do. my parents were thousands of miles away and I had no one to talk to about what just happened. I got back on the ferry to go home and walked the 3 miles home. when I got home, I emailed my parents and told them what had happened and waited. I paced the house, rocked, jumped, moaned and so on. it took what felt like forever but was only a half hour or so before they phoned. I whimpered while I told them what had happened me getting arrested for theft and feeling so out of control. they told me to stay at home they would call one of our friends and get them over their to help me and stay with me and they would take the first flight back home and would deal with what has happened. While I waited for the friend to get their I scratched my arms and dug my nails into my fists. I was really out of control and was having thoughts of hurting myself and or killing myself. When the friend got their I was really wound up and quenching my fists into tight balls with the nails digging into my skin so hard they were starting to bleed. They took one look at me and phoned my parents and said I was in bad shape and they were afraid to be around me. My parents suggested to get me to want to go to the hospital into the psych ward. So, they asked if I wanted to go to the hospital and I said yes. So, they called 911 and told the operator to send a ambulance and gave the address that they had a young man that wants to go to the hospital and is acting like a danger to himself and others. The police shoed up 10 minutes later and did a search and pat down of me to make sure I was safe to transport. Then the ambulance came, and I got in and they took me to the hospital that was in the city so yet another ferry ride but this time in a hospital. I got to the hospital and they made me wait for ever. I had to give them a pee sample so they could do a test on it and find out what I was on that was making me crazy. I told them that I was their for a detox that the drug quesertan was to blame and that I just needed a couple of days to detox and I would be fine. it took 5 hours to get admitted to the psych ward and get a bed, so it was after 10 by this time and i just wanted to sleep. they were supposed to give me something for me to sleep and calm down, but they never did. I did not get any sleep that night and the next day was pretty rough on me. I got to so a psych doc and he researched it and said it was the quesertan that caused it that it is bad for people with autism or psychotic tendencies. he prescribed an anti-psychotic med Risperidone and Ativan plus omega 3. the Ativan is for the panic attacks. the risperidone is for the voices and such. the omega 3 is to help keep the brain connections working properly. I stayed their for 3 days and then my parents got their and talked to the doc and he said if they wanted to they could take me home so they discharged me and I went home. It took 6 months, but I was able to get my job back at work I just was not allowed to work with cash. I could just stock the shelves and answer customers questions. I got off with the charge of theft because it was not my fault it was the herbal med that I was on that caused the problem. so, all I had

to do was pay them back and write a apology letter

with a essay on how much companies loose in

employee theft. So, I did that, and all is good.

Chapter 7

As far as I can remember

As far as I can remember and what my parents have

told me I did not do much walking till I was 3 and

even then, I tripped over my feet a lot of the time.

Plus, I would bump into stuff all the time. I always

had bruises on me from all the stuff I would walk

into. I got my first set of glasses at the age of 3 so it

did help that I could see a bit better. As far as I can

remember and what my parents have told me I did
not do much talking till I was 3 or more. I was a
nonverbal till then and even after I did not say much
or use many words to say it. I just liked to observe people and
did not want to talk to them. I did not see the point in it because
I was getting everything, I needed without having to say much
or at all.

As far as I can remember and what my parents have told me I
did not do much crawling till about 20 months of age and when
I did crawl, I would crawl like a crab. I would push myself off
the ground by my feet and hands and then move them in a crab
like movement. they said they were always amazed at how fast
I could move doing crab like crawling.

I am so used to my anxiety that most of the time I do not even
notice it. I am social phobic, clostic phobic (phobic of enclosed

spaces), and afraid of stuff happening to me at any given moment that could hurt

me or kill me. I am afraid to go outside or go anywhere. I am afraid even at home of something happening to me. I hate how much anxiety that I feel and have to go through. I cannot seem to get people like my parents or my doctors to understand how much anxiety that I have. they don't want me on meds for it and I really could use some meds for it. I cannot stand to feel like this it is crippling my life and I am not able to do basic life functions as a result of how bad it is for me. I am afraid of everything you could possibly imagine happening all the time. Please just make it stop I cannot live like this.

You do learn how to better handle different

situations the more times you have to go through

them. I am multiple times better now than I used to

 be for having outbursts and walking away. It just

takes time to learn the skills necessary to be able to handle

them.

I was quite old when I started to blow my nose. Late teen years I think. I used to just rub it on my sleeves or snort it up again and swallow it. I always have phlegm stuck in my throat bugging the hell out of me. I have never got the hang of getting rid of the phlegm. I just keep trying to swallow it.

I am really shy in person and in new situations and also get really frustrated when I am unable to do things as well as I would like to. I am way different online then in person in person I would never be able to do all this communicating. I would not be able to do this on the phone or Skype either only by email or text am I this out going.

I just do not like to be cornered. I always need a

escape plan a way out that is why being around lots of people is so hard for me and I have to put myself into a place that is easy to escape from.

Chapter 8

My other issues

When I was little, I was really shy and really hyperactive. I also had really prominent ears that stuck way out. I had surgery to fix the ears when I was 5 years old.

I always do a lot of hand flapping when I get excited and the more excited, I get the faster I flap my hands.

I always want to know what to expect in any given situation so that I can be prepared to react fast if I need to. If I am caught off guard, it can take me a long time to react and that can get me into trouble. That is why I do not like change in routine because it means that I do not know what to expect and usually get myself into trouble as a result.

I always have to watch myself that I don't start scratching myself because if I start it is hard for me to stop. It feels so good to scratch myself that I get carried away and scratch till I ooze and bleed. I usually scratch my arms, feet, nose, and crotch. Whatever is closest and itching the most gets my attention at that time. On my feet I use anti-fungal cream to stop the itching and it works good for stopping it.

It is better to know lots about a select few subject then know little about lots of subjects. That is why I like to be fixed on a few subjects that I like.

I squint at everything even if it is not bright out. I think it is to limit the amount of visual information going to the brain to stop an overload. I tend to close my eyes when my picture is being taken because I am afraid of the flash the camera makes.

I have terrible depth perception and special awareness and cannot tell how far anything is from me or how fast it is traveling towards me. As a result, I was terrible at sports especially ones where stuff was hurtled at me. Like almost all the sports out they're except golf and bowling. The only problem with golf is that I can't tell how far or where my ball went so, I have to have someone looking for me for where it went.

when I get really anxious, I get bad ticks and loss of muscle control. My face muscles start jumping around and so does my shoulder muscles. It is really annoying.

I have the hyper-extensible joints and my joints get dislocated all the time. In fact, I tend to crack almost every joint in my body at one time or another jurying each and every day.

I have a heart murmur that causes me some problems because it does not pump at a regular beat, so the oxygen does not get to my muscles in a regular time frame, so they get weak a lot of the time.

I used to memorize all the fairy tales my parents used to say to me every night and they thought that I could read too but I could not I was just pretending to.

I have an amazing memory. My parents treat me like a encyclopedia for movies, tv shows, books, computers and the like.

Really any type of distraction from what is causing me to have my meltdown helps but music is the best for me. I like tv shows, movies and audio books for this too but music is still the best for me.

I am beter at algebra or trigonometry then any basic math. It took me three years to figure out how to do geometry.

I once in grade 8 figured out how many nano seconds a person would live if they lived to 100 years old and I did it all over lunch break by hand with no calculator. Do you realize how big a number that is. there are 100 nano seconds in a millisecond, 100 milliseconds in a second, 60 seconds in a minute, 60 minutes in a hour, 24 hours in a day, 7 days in a week, 30.44 days in a month, 52 weeks in a year, 365.25 days in a year, for 100 years. that is one hell of a large number and I figured it out in 40 minutes.

Becoming really good at something has helped me a lot. I am really good at computers in fact I am a certified computer technician and graduated with a 95% overall grade from collage. I only got my grade 10 but graduated from collage figure that one out. I work at Literacy Nanaimo refurbishing old computers to give to families on welfare. So, I really like my job now and am really good at it.

I loved the lion king movies too. I even got so obsessed with them that I made a movie script for a sequel called the return of the lions. and sent in to them at the Disney company. They sent a polite page back saying that they have their own people to come up with ideas for sequels but that I could join the summer acting camp they do every year in Hollywood and see if acting is something that I would want to get into. My parents thought it was so sweat of them. I was pretty disappointed though.

My parents and the school made me every sport there is I even tried ice hockey. It was not till I was 12 and found bowling and golf that I finally found 2 sports that I could actually get some what good at. I play golf with my parents every once in a while, and go bowling only on special occasions.

I like to play golf, but I cannot see where the ball goes so I need someone to keep a lookout for where it lands.

I do not get many strikes, but I do tend to get a lot of spares in bowling. I like that I am somewhat good at at least 2 sports.

it is good that I can play those sports so that I get some exercise and outside socializing done.

My parents started me in karate on my 8th birthday and I continued with it till we moved when I was 12. They felt it would be good for me to build some muscle and try to help me defend myself from all the bullying that was happening to me. I got to the third to last belt that they gave out the blue belt. Only the brown, and black belts were above mine so that was pretty good for me.

They thought that I would make some friends their also but alas that was not the case all the other kids hatted me because I would not put up a good fight when we spared.

What they did not know is that I was holding back because I was afraid of hurting them.

I got pretty good at all the katas and drills that I had to do. I could jump over object to kick someone. I could break boards with my fists and with kicks. I got to play with wooden swords and num-chucks and learn ninja moves because I was the best behaved in the class. That does not say much about the rest of the class mind you.

I went twice a week for 5 years but once we moved it was too hard to stay in the class and so I had to stop going.

Washing cloths changes how they feel, smell, the colours change. Also, how warm or cold the clothes make me feel can impact me wanting to wear it or not. I do not like wearing different clothes every day, so I wear the same thing for a week and then wash it. I usually have only two sets of clothes to wear for each season so when I do have to wash my one set, I can just put on the second set. I hate wearing different clothes every day it is so hard to get used to the clothes that I wear for a week let alone have to get adjusted to new clothes every day that would drive me nuts.

I used to watch the French channel when they had

 the same cartoons that I usually watch to see what

they were like in French and they usually were very

funny indeed. I did not really learn French through it, but it was

funny to listen to the French dialog.

I was in a sink or swim school that did not pass you if you

could not do the work and get at least a 50% grade. I wanted

very much to pass and stay with my classmates.

I was never better than a C student but at least I passed.

I got an exercise routine and have been using it for

years and years and years with no luck. I went to the

gym and did workouts especially for the knees and

did them 3 times a week for 2 years and still with no

luck. All my effort at the gym would ware off in a

 day and I worked out for over an hour each time I

went and the results just never happened. I do not

think that my muscles are able to strengthen. They

are missing some key ingredient to make the muscles retain the

workout.

When I was little, I thought it would be better to be a dog then

a boy so I started to act like a dog. I stopped walking and would

only crawl. I stopped talking and would only bark. I stopped

poty training and would just go when ever. I stopped eating at

the table and would only eat on the floor and so on. I did this

for over a month till my parents had had it and grounded me

with no food till

l I started to act like a boy again. Thinking back on

it it was a really strange thing to do because I gave

up watching TV, playing games, or with my toys, I

gave up everything to do with being a boy and only

did stuff that a dog would do. I dug in dirt, sniffed

peoples buts, used my feet to scratch myself, laid

around and slept where ever I felt like it. I even stopped

sleeping in my bed and just slept on the ground next to my bed.

I would not use my hands for anything including eating. I

would drink out of a bowl like a dog and eat like a dog without

using my hands just biting at the food. It must have looked

really funny for a while for my parents to see me go to such

lengths to be a dog. I got over it but would occasionally act like

a dog for a afternoon till I turned 8. To this day I still cannot

see why I did it but I guess at the time I felt it was easier to be a

dog then be me with all the problems that I had to face that a

dog really does not have to face.

I would get up at 5 in the morning every morning till

I started grade 1 and turn on the TV and flip

through the channels till I found some cartoons to

watch and would watch them till my mom would

come for me to eat some breakfast. Even after starting grade 1 I would do it on Saturdays and Sundays. I was 13 before I started to sleep in all the time and even then, it was just to 8 or 9 and get up and watch some cartoons on TV.

I watch crime TV shows and medical dramas. I play virtual hockey games and watch hockey on TV. I blog about what it was like growing up as me. I read fantasy books and listen to their audio books. I play strategy games on the computer and fiddle with the computer to try and keep it in perfect working order. That is what I do these days to make me happy.

I repeat TV lines and quote TV lines in conversations. I re watch movies and TV shows many many times too. My parents cannot understand how I can watch the same stuff over and over again. But I always like to watch the stuff I like as many times as I can.

I used to watch all my favourite cartoons in French because I found the different sounds that French makes compared to English fascinating. I never got good at other languages, but I always liked to listen to them.

I never had YouTube to do it with, but I would probably have done the same thing. I learned to count to 20 in French in school but that is as far as I got.

I had too much trouble with English that the school decided not to bother with French by grade 4.

I love bouncing on balls it is so much fun. I do a bit of jumping but not much of it. I visibly shake when I am anxious enough and have muscle spasms.

when I was little, we had no videos to watch so I would just turn on the TV and flip though the channels till I found some cartoons to watch. I did that for years till I had to start grade 1 and needed my sleep.

when I was little, we only had 12 channels, so it was not hard to find the cartoons. they were only on one or two channels and I memorized which channels they were and would just go to them. It is harder now with so many channels to choose from.

I always thought of myself as a genius because of my good memory till I realized that it does not help you get or keep a job.

I love rocking in rocking chairs it is so soothing and bouncing on beds is so much fun. I used to have a water bed and loved the rolling motion that the water made when I moved around on it. I really miss my water bed there is nothing as good as a water bed for a good night sleep

 I think it is sort of hypnotic in a way because when i am rocking I do not think and just let my mind wonder and it is so good not to have to think about what i should be doing or saying or feeling. I could rock for hours just like I can pet my dog for hours and have a similar effect of just drifting away and letting all my feelings and emotions and stresses melt away from me for just a little while.

I have been on a lot of boats and ferries and never have felt sea sick. I live on a small island of 4000 and have to take a ferry to a city of 100 000 and it get pretty rough in the winter so sea sickness does not affect me in fact I kind of enjoy the rocking motion of the ferry and could sleep really easily on a boat.

I am learning so much from the ASD groups. I went more

than 17 years not knowing about it so it is all pretty knew to

me. As they say if you don't know something is wrong then

you don't know that you should not be able to do it. So you

just do it as best you can and move on. It can hold you back if

 you think that you should be and act a certain way. I say just

be yourself and hope for the best. You never know what will come your

way to help you make the most of your life.

Those so-called experts told my parents that

 I would have to be put in a group home and

never let out. They said that I would never be

 able to go to college, get my driver's licence (I am

still working on that one),

get a job of meaningful value. They said I

would never live on my own (I am still

working on that one) That I would never amount to anything and to not waste their time and not to bother trying. I am so glad my parents and me did not listen to what the experts said my life would be like. What do those experts know anyways they never had to deal with ASD so till they have they will never know how much is possible if you just try hard enough to make it happen.

the best thing you can do is limit the stimuli that is around them. Work with him in a quiet place without distractions and one on one make them have to focus on you and talk to them and name items. Only bring one item in at a time and name it over and over again in between talking to them.

I had no therapy of any kind growing up, but my mom was a stay at home mom till I was 12 and then went to work part time and at 13 started full time.

I would love to meet anyone that is in the ASD community and visit and answer their questions and such maybe one day I can make it to a conference and be a speaker and make it happen.

Because I have only been on the Asperger's group for a couple of weeks not too many people know about me, but I am getting a lot more people wanting to talk to me every day and I do not mind since I do not have a job anymore so can focus my efforts on this.

when you stand you are touching the ground
 and for me I can feel every little thing that

every little bit of my feet touches.

Kids used to poke me in the stomach as some type of game but it hurt so much, I would instantly smack their hand away and hit them hard back in their stomach area. They stopped doing it to me pretty quickly after that.

I really do not like to be tickled even if it feels good it feels to overwhelming and I make it stop if it goes on for more than a minute because it is too much stimulus for me to handle. I get a quick scare if I get touched and am not expecting it and will lash out at whoever touched me. I do not mean to do it it is just instinctual and cannot be stopped. It is like what

would you do if someone slapped you the common response is
to slap back. You probably don't even think about it you just do
it it is the same with this.

I never let people know that I can do something till I have to do
it in front of them. I learned to read when I was 5 but could not
read out loud for fear of making a mistake in the pronunciation
of the words even though I could read them. I was never called
that, but I was never called anything other than a teachers best
student because i did not ask for any help ever. the first thing I
got good at writing was my name also.

or my computer classes I read every book on the

subject and memorized them but for early

education My mom worked with me for hours every

day doing fun counting. naming, doing my ABC's, working
with me for spelling tests drills, and flash cards. I cannot think
of the stuff that worked or not.

I never felt as outta control as I did as a teenager. It was all that pent-up sexual energy that I did not know what to do with. I do not think that there is good way to get through puberty and the teen years. they are the toughest on everybody.

I just do not like to be cornered. I always need a escape plan a way out that is why being around lots of people is so hard for me and I have to put myself into a place that is easy to escape from.

Well as for relationships I have had lots of friends

over the years and I have even had several girl

friends over the years so it is possible to have

relationships. As for having kids of their own I

would not recommend it because they will just pass

this on to their kids. I was never really violent till I

stated puberty and my teen years. I never realized if

I was being violent or what it was doing to the people around me.

starting at 2.5 yo of age I had a 8pm bedtime and I would get

my fairy tales told to me at that time and then go to bed. I

always got up at 5am to watch TV though. I would wake up

much earlier than when I finally would get up. I did not want to

wake my parents up which were just across the hall from me. I

had a mid-day nap though through pre-school and kindergarten.

I did not actually nap during

that time but I did decompress and used the time to recuperate

from all the stimuli. I did not take any meds till I was 16.5 to

17.5 and then not again till I was 28.5.

Chapter 9

Summery

Even though having ASD is hard at times I would not be who I am without it and I like who I am. I have my challenges and have issues that I deal with on a daily basses but I do have a job that I go to 4 days a week 4 hours a day and I like it a lot plus it gives me something to do and I do not think that I could do much more then that amount of hours.

I don't mind the living situation that I am in living with a support worker and another gentleman that is disabled also. I get fed each and every day and they are really good meals and he helps with doctor's appointments and advocates for me to get me the best support that I can get.

I have a support person that I see in the community that takes me out to yoga, walks, shopping and anything else that I want to do. I have them 3 days a week for 3 hours a day so that gives me lots of time to do the things I want during the week. I see them Mondays, Thursdays, and Fridays.

I work Tuesdays through to Fridays at the library putting books away and sorting the selves making sure that all the books are in the right order.

I like my life and I think that you can live a most normal life with having ASD. There is hope and there is a future for those on the ASD spectrum. More and more companies are hiring people with ASD seeing the up side of having a person with ASD on their staff.

I hope that this book has been helpful for you and that you see how your ASD person can have a somewhat normal life. There is hope for those on the ASD spectrum to get a job and keep it plus live in semi-independent living. Be able to save for their retirement and have spending money to buy things that they want to buy to support there special interests.

This is a preview of the book that I am working on hope you enjoy.

The Mystical World of Magic

CHAPTER ONE
The Boy and his Pain

He was running down a rode with four people running after him. There was not much time they were gaining and were now only thirty feet away. They all had thire hands ready to grab him and drag him to the ground. He scampered down a ally way which was a short cut to get him home quicker. The sound of the four came around the corner with such speed than one of them fell over their feet in the hast to take the corner. The folen one jumped up and with a scoul on his face got up and continued the pursit. They were gaing on him and he was still far away from his home. 'after him you idiots' was herd in the distance as he ran up another rode and down another allyway. "Im not far now" thought the boy as he ran yet agin down another street. Just then he was hit right over his head with a big crack. The group of people how had been following him had found a way to get infront of him by taking a different ally and ended up impairing his path. He looked up with such horer as he saw what hat hit him that he screamed for help but no one came to his aid. The tallest and toufest boy looked down at him and said to his fellow boys 'get him up and bind his arms while I beat the snot out of him.' The three other boys did what he said smirking and sounding gleefull all at what was coming next. The big one then spent the next ten minutes dong what he said he was going to do to the boy. After it was done the four boys walked off talking about the look on the boys face when the first punch hit his nose.

The boy looked in a right mess laying on the ground his nose broken, eyes black and blue, glases bent in odd sorts of ways, and blood skirting out of his broken nose. He picked his distorted glasses off the ground and put them back on his busted nose so that he could see. He looked around but no one was anywhere to be seen. So he got to his feet verry slowly as he hurt all over and started slowly towards his house again pinching his nose so as to try and slow down the bleeding from his nose.

He was a skinny mid hight boy with glasses and soft red
hair. His jeans were riped, had wholes in his nees, his hair
roufelld and stiking out all over the place. The shirt he wore
was blood staind, wrinkled and torn and the neck seem. He
was a twelve year old boy with the look that a mob of people
had ploued over him. He walked slowly along the rode
muttering to him self 'I'll get them for this' or 'how dare them
do this to me' under his breath in turns. The four that had
done this to him were noware to be found now and it was
perficly safe for him to talk freely now that they were gone.
He strolled up his drive way ten minutes latter with a look of
anguise on his face, because he would have to deal with his
parents when he opened the door. He got to the dore and
with a last 'beter get this over with' he opened the door.
His mom was waiting for him with a what happened to you
now sort of look about her. This was a weekly event in this
house and he always lied saying anything but what was
actuly going on so not to get his parents involved.

'what happened to you this time boy' she said with a note of impatience in her voice because she expeteed that he was lying to her about what was happeing to him. 'I fell down the stairs at school' he said while looking at the ground. 'really is that your story this time is it' his mom said to him unconvinced. 'Yea it was a nasty fall too, triped over my feet and fell down ten stairs to hit the wall with my nose' said the boy still picning his nose to stop the bleeding. 'Come here then, while I put your nose back into place and bandage you up' came his moms voice while she steped over to him and helped him into a chiar at the dinning room table. She then said 'it is going to hurt when I put your nose back in so hold on.' She then took her nose in her hand and broke it back into positing so it could start to heal itself. 'Just wait till your farther hears about his newest injury to your self' his mom told him in a stern sort of way. His stomach lurched at this news 'Your going to tell him but it was just a stopid fall why should he need to know about it'. 'he' began his mom in a tired voice 'needs to know because you get your self hert at least once a week and your story seems a bit fishy if you ask me'. 'Fishy' the boy said shaking alitle as he did. 'Fishy yes indeed' said his mom. 'But that's what happend alright' he said getting a little upset at his mom for proding him for information. 'You don't really expect me to belive that you fell down a stair case and got that badly hert doing it. You have got to be kiding' his mom said to him. 'Why does it matter anyway it will all heal and all, so what is their to get so upset at.' He said really strting to get upset now by his mom constent jabbering at him and just wanting to be in his room alone.

'Oh all right then, go to your room and don't come out of there till I come for you.' His mom said with such furry she knocked over one of the chairs at the table and it went crash to the floor. He ran from the room up the stair case in into his room which was on the right when he got to the top of the stairs and slmed his door on the way into his room. He couldn't belived his mother had acted that way to him and knew it was not going to be a good night in this house tonight. He slouched on his bed just hopeing it would all be over soon and he could sleep it off.

He lived in a nice house on a rode called Bramberry Street. The house was number 49 and was hid because of all the fur trees that surrounded the place. It was a nice size two story plus a besment with four bedrooms, three bathrooms, a living and family room, kitchein, dinning room, and a office of sorts. It had a big treed back yard, with a tree house, a play house, and a swing set.

His parents were good people and always looked after him to the best of their ability. He had a yonger brother which he had never met because he was adopted at the age of one. The parents he had now were his adopted parents but they had never told him that he was adopted till last summer.

He lay on this bed thinking about the summer holidays which were only a month away. He liked the summer time better then any other time of the year. This was because he could avoid the bullies much more easily when he was not in school.

It was a worm and breasy late may day, the floweres were blooming, the birds were chirping, kids were laphing and having a good time in the background. Yet he was laying on his bed beaten and swollen all over his body.

He did not mind laying on his bed as it was very relaxing and he did not have the energy to do anything else. He thought to himself about what he was going to do this summer. Was he going to go and have a swim at the lake which was just a mile away from his house and was a easy walk to make. Or was he going to go to his favorite tree by the ocean front and lay around their getting a sun tan.

He sure needed a sun tan because he was a very bleak looking boy with white bloched legs and arms. His hair was soft red and always looked a bit messy but it did not matter what he did to his hair it never quite looked right.

He could hear a car drive in the driveway and new that his dad was home from work for the day. He could hear the house door open and hear him walking in and talking with his wife. He sounded like he had, had a bad day at work and just wanted to sit down and have super in peace.

His dad was a big man with matted black hair and a body of a boxer. He was the type of man you new not to try and fight because it would be a lost cause. He worked at a floor covering store as the manajor and head sealsmen. He was pretty good at what he did and kept them all fed, clothed and housed because of it.

He new he would be having the talk to with his dad in just a few minuets. He did not care though, he was so upset now it did not matter what his dad did to him at this point. His dad was going to go though the same talk he gave him every Friday at this time. There was really no way to get out of it so he midswell get it over with.

He rolled off his bed and headed slowly to the bedroom door. Out he went from it and down the hall to the stairs. Then he perseded down the stairs and headed for the dinning room. When he got to the dinning room he said 'hello' to his mom and dad that were seated there already.

   His father looked over at him with a look of discust on his face and said 'Not again boy! I think it is time I had a little chat with your teacher at school. I don't care what you told your mother but you did not fall down a stair case to get that much injury. You look like you were stampeded or something.'

   Honest all I did was fall down some stairs. Why do you need to get the school involved for a stupied thing like that. Im just clumsy that's all no need to get them involved.

   'Oh yes there is need!' His dads rising voice came at him. 'If you ask me you look like you have been in a huge scrum and you came out the worst for ware.'

   'If you get the school involed it will only get worse! Yelled the boy

'So you admit it do you! That you are getting into fist fights every week.'

'I didn't say that!' the boy snaped back

'Don't you talk to me that way boy!' His dad spat back

'I don't want to talk about it! Came the boys voice

'Jeremy Evens Sabation Smith go to your room you are grounded for a month. No telly, no phone, no friends, and no supper tonight! You will not be allowed out of your room for anything exept to have meals, go to the bathroom and go to school!' His dads voice rang at the top of his voice. Making his wife to fall off her chair in the prosess.

   'Fine!' said Jeremys voce as he jumped to his feet and stormed up to his room slaming the door as he entered it.

CHAPTER TWO

The Grounding

He woke up next morning still furious at what his dad had done last night. He was not looking forward to what he would be doing in his room with nothing to do. He new it would be better than having to go to school, which he hated with a passen.

He got up and went out of his room to the bathroom. Their he started a bath and took a leak in the jon while he was at it. When his bath was ready he took off all of his clothes and got it.

The walter was nice and warm on his cold skin and he started to sope himself up to get clean. This he figerd was going to be the only fun thing he would be doing all day so he stayed in their for close to an hour.

His dad finely came looking for him and got him out of the tub, dried and sent him back to his room so fast it happened in a blur of couler.

He sat on his bed for another hour when finnaly he was called down to lunch by his dad.

He walked down to the dinning room where he would finnaly have his first meal in twenty four hours.

'Im starved whats for lunch.' He said in a tired soft voice. 'Baken, eggs, hashbrons, toast, and a glass of oj.' Came his moms voice from the kitchen while she was cooking it.
'Sounds delishes.' He said rubbing his growling stomach.
'Yes it sure does.' His dad said looking over his newspaper to check the sights.

The meal was the best he had had for a long time he thought to himself. He was glad that he got to eat because he was so very hungry indeed. He cleaned off his plate of any food before heading back up to his room till he was allowed to come down to have his supper.

*

His dads name was Aurthor Leminton Sabation Smith and his moms name was Lilly Rebeca Evens Smith. They could not have children of their own so they adopted young Jeremy at the age of one. They lived in a small town called Rockford. There are only five thousand people that live in the town. It is only a hours dirve to a city of seventy thousand.

It only had one elementy school and one high school for the kids to go to. They had to go to the city to go to college and university. There was only two hundred students that whent to the two schools each. So the class sizes were a little bit smaller than that of the city.

Jeremy hated school so very much indeed. He was twelve years old and most of the way though grade six getting half desent grades but he was scroney, weak and got picked on all the time. He wished that he could defend himself but every time he tried to he just got a extra long beating.

*

The next month flew by with a blur of colurs and events. Of course the beatings still acoured once a week and the lecures folled each one of them. Jeremy was glad that it was the last day of school before the summer holidays and he would soon have some time to heal before school started up again in September. It would be a whole two months before he would get beaten up agiain by the four boys.

The last day of school was a plesent one spent cleaning
everything up and watching a movie before being dismissed
for the summer. Jeremy new that it was going to be a
challenge getting home in one piece because of the four boys
that were surly going to pound on him on his way home. The
only good thing was that he would not see them for two
whole months which made him very happy indeed.

He rose from his seat, put his backpack on his back and
strode out of his classroom into the buseling hallway. He was
emeditly swept away with the croud to the front doors and
out into the neat kept lawn of his school.

He then headed strait towards the nearest street that would
take him back to his house the quickest. He new he would not
have much time before he would be chased at top speed by
the four boys. He turned down the rode and started to walk
quite fast but very quietly indeed. He turned left down a
allyway and continued to pick up speed as he went. He
turned right at the next street and was in a half jog when he
saw to his horror the four boys running after him down the
rode. 'Where do you think your going in such a hurry.'
Screeched the biggest boy who was leading the others at a
run. Jeremy ignored it and started running himself swerved
and turned left down another allyway.

The boys were not too far behind him and he still had a far
way to go. He was not going to be able to get away they were
to close. He put on a huge burst of speed and ran as fast has
his legs would handle.

He turned right and flew down another rode and then left
again down another ally. Still with the boys running after him
but they were getting further away because they just could not
run as fast as he was running. He had a stich in his side now
though and he figered he would only beable to keep it up for
maybe another minete or two at the most.

Two minetes later he finaly had to slow down to a slow jog
because he just could not keep up the speed that he had been
doing. He new the boys were still after him because he could
here there pounding steps in the far distance. He had three
blocks left if he hurried he might just make it home before
they caught up to him.

'Must keep going, only a few more blocks and im home
free.' He said outloud as he forced himself to keep half runing
down the street. The boys were slowly catching up to him
and it was only a matter of time before they did. He was not
going to make it to his house in time.

A few more minutes passed with the boys still a fair way
behind him and he thought to himself that he might acualy
make it. He than heard their foot steps behind him and he
looked over his shoulder to see how far away they were. They
were only a half block away now and he was still over a block
away so he new he was not going to make it.

He stoped running having had enough of running from
them and turned to face his enemies. He through off his back
pack and it landed on the other side of the ditch on a soft
grassy area. He stood waiting for them to catch up with him
so that he could get it over with.

It seemed like a long time that he stood there stairing down
the street at the four that were aproching. He was going to
fight them this time and maybe even win for once he thought
to himself. He saw them aproch him and stop right infront of
him blocking the whole rode.

'So you have finaly stoped running and are going to let us
beat the crap out of you!' Came the biggest of the fours voice
through clenched teeth.

'Im not going to let you beat me up, Im going to fight you!'
Jeremy shouted back at him.

'Did you hear that boys' The big one laghed allowed 'hes
going to try and fight us.'

The others all started to lagh also and it made Jeremy very
upset.

'Stop laghing I am going to fight back, Iv had enough of you guys beating on me! I will not take it any more!' Jeremy said with such fury in his voice as he had never felt before about anyting.

'Boys I think we should teach Germy what happenes to people that fight back shall we!' The leader said as he cracked his nuckels.

'Just try it, Im ready for ya!' yelled Jeremy as he got into a fighting stance ready to fight back.

'Get him boys!' screeched the leader to the other three.

The three boys circeled Jeremy with the look of a pack of wolves hunting their pray waiting for the perfect moment to strike. Jeremy was calculating every move they could make and was getting ready to counter it. He new the boys were tough but they were not very bright and that was his strength was that he was bright and could easily tell what they were going to do before they did it.

The leader of the gane was looking pretty pleased with the way things were going and seemed to think that he had won the fight even before the first punch was thouen. He new his openent and new that he was no match for four big tough guys punding him so there was no match between his gane and his openent. He had him right where he wanted him and he was ready to strike.

The boys were in position and were ready to stike all they needed was their leaders orders to strike. They waited pationenly for those orders as they circled their pray. It was almost time now and they could taste the sweet smell of a good fight on their lips.

"Now boys strike him hard and get this over with!"
The three boys rushed the center one and pounced. All three of them haled the one to the ground and started hitting every inch that they could find of him.

The boy at the bottom of the pile started to feel a surge of energy like he had never felt before in his entire life. It started from the middle of his chest and spred rapidly. What was also strange was that he could not feel anything. He was in no pain at all and was in perfect helth to bout.

The energy build up was gitting massive now. He could feel it pulsate though his body and it was beging to make him glow. He had never felt like this before and did not know what to expect.

Then whith a towering pulse of energy the three boys that were trying to hit him were blasted twenty feet away from him. They landed with a terrible crash in the ditches and did not get up. They had been knocked uncountious by the force of the crash.

Jeremy noticed that he had electricity shoting out of his hands for several inches in every direction from them. He stood up and looked first at his hands and then at the leader of the gane which was still standing infront of him wide eyed and looking terrified.

"You want some of that." Jeremy said with a shakey voice to the boy in front of him.

The boy took off running in the opisite direction of the boy leving his gane members to lay where they landed.

CHAPTER THREE

The Awakening

Jeremy did not quite understand what had happened but he new that he should get out of there before someone saw the three boys laying in the ditches unconsis. He quickly looked around to make sure no one was watching and then started off towards his home.

"What had happened? How did I do that?" he said outloude to himself as he was walking home. It was the weirdest thing he had ever experienced in his life.

Time passed by as he slowly walked down the roads. His mind racing the whole time trying to comprehend what had taken place. He did not even look to see where he was going and when he did look up he was already infront of his driveway.

He walked up it and opened the front door. Then walked inside and closed it again.

"Jeremy where have you been!" came his moms voice as she walked to the front door with a stearn look on her face.

"Iv been walking home slowly enjoying the start of summer vacation." Jeremy said in a drowsy voice.

"Get to your room and stay there till you are called for." His mom said as she escorted him to his room.

He was glad that he got to stay in his room and not have to talk to anyone. He just wasn't in the mood after what he had experienced. He went over to his bed and flopped down on it.

He started thinking about everything that had happened today and was trying to figure out what it all means. 'How did I through those boys off of me. I don't even remember touching them.' He thought to himself while staring at the celing.

He was trying to remember every little bit of detail of the event so as to figure out some explanation of what had happened. He could not find anything that even remotly made any sence to him. 'It had all happened so fast.' He thought to himself. The event had lasted less than a minute, even if it seemed like it had lasted a long time.

He got up and then started pacing around his room trying to modevate his brain to think faster. It was just making it worse for him so he flooped back onto his bed and stared at the celing again.

Just an hour before if somebody had tried to tell him that he was going to cause three bigger kids to fly off of him and crash unconsice in the nearby ditches he would have said they were mad and to get lost. As it stood, he had done that event, and was now trying to make sence of it all.

'What did it all mean? Was their really power behond anything that you could possibly imaging and how far dose that power go? How much could he do with it and would he ever use it again?' plaged his mind as he thought about everything that had happened.

He than realized something, he had asked for the ability to never again have to wory about being hurt again. He had not asked outloud but in his head for it. He had not expedted for anything to happen though. It seemed that his wish was answered and he was given the power needed to stop the hurting. He did not know what power he had been given but he was now very thankfull to have gotten it when he did.

He herd his door open and his mom walked in saying "Time for supper young man, no tataling this time." She walked out of the room but left the door open so that Jeremy would have to get up. Which really anoued him as he hated when people leave the door open.

He got up and slowly headed for the door and out of the room. The smell of the food cooking was wafting up the stairs and it smellt so very good indeed. Walked down the stairs two at a time to find out what was cooking and rounded the corner into the dinning room and then on to the kitchen.
"That sure smells good. What are you cooking anyway?" Jeremy asked as he looked in on the cooking. "It is lazona with mashed potato and rosted carots." Came his moms voice as she hurried around trying to get everything ready so that they could eat.
They ate supper in silence for the longest time till her mom spoke up "You really don't look well Jeremy what happened to you on your walk home? You don't look like you were hurt but you look pale and weak looking."
"Nothing happened mom Im fine." Jeremy said in a discustfull tone of voice. He was not in the mood to talk to his mom or dad about what had happened earlier that day. Even if he had wanted to they would not be able to understand anyway.
"I don't belive you young man and I don't think your father does either." His mom said while giving her son a pircing stare that made the hairs of Jeremy's neck stand on end with their feicness.
His father spoke for the first time that evning to him "I have to agree with your mother Jeremy you do look ill at that." His tone had a tinge of niceness in it because for the first time in a long time his son had gotten home with out getting hurt but his son did not look any better than if he had gotten hurt.
"It's just been a long day and all I need is a good night sleep." Jeremy said with a tired expression on his face. He was tired after all, so he wasent lying too badly. What ever had throuen those boys off of him had draind him considerably and all he wanted to do was have a good night sleep.
"May I go to bed then." He said to his parents looking both of them in the eyes.

"I see why not, we can relook in to this in the morning." His mom said. "I think that is fair." Said his dad.
"Good night mom and same to you dad."
"Good night." His partents said to him as he got to his feet and walked dragging his feet to the staircase.
Slowly he dragged his feet up the staris. It was taking for ever but eventually, which seemed like a long time but was actually only about two minuets, he got to the top of the sairs. Then he walked though the opening to his room and closed the door behind him.
He took off his close with quite some effort and got slowly but surley into his pj's and into bed. He was quite glad to be in bed under his covers where it felt safe and protected. He fell asleep within minutes.
It was a stormy night, the wind was blazing, the trees were swaying, and there was genuine unease in the air. The forces were changing all around the area and increadible power was building up near by. Something strange and unusual was stirring around. Something that had not stired in over three hundred years.
It was verry dark out side and only the trees were making any noise. It was a new moon and all was in darkness because of it. Little did they know that danger and evil were coming to haunt their doorstep.

Chapter 4

The New abilities

The sun was the first thing that Jeremy saw when he opened his eyes. It was streaming though his blinds and eliminated his room with a soft glow. He slid out of the covers, got to his feet and strolled to his door. When he opened it he had to sqint for a while because it was too bright for his eyes. Once they had adjusted to the brightness of the hallway he continued down to the kitchen to get something to eat. "good morn" he said to his mom that was in the kitchen making some coffee. "So you finaly decided to join the civilization and get out of bed" said his mom with a sarcastic touch too it. Jeremy slouched over to the fridge and got himself a glass of orange juice then he grabed his favorite cereal and pored himself a boul full after that he sat down and started to have his brekfest. He tought to himself I have got to get out of the house and try to get someware privet where I can figger things out. He finnised his brekfest as fast as he could and put his dishes in the dishwasher.

"Im going out I will be back at supper time." Came Jeremy's voice from the front door.
"Ok but be carfull and be home before six" Said his mother from the kitchen.
Jeremy grabed his coat put on his shoes and left the house. He headed to his school where there was a large forest behind it with a clearing in the middle which makes a good hiding place.
When he got to the clearing he sat down at the bottom of a big spruce tree.

He thought to himself 'There must be an explemation for what is happening to me. I can't begoing mad can I. No I think not, I know what I saw and it was of a power I have never seen.'

He sat there for hours and hours thiking it all over when finaly he said 'Well all I can think of is to try and do some more magic and see what happendes.'

He got up off the ground and brushed off all the dirt that was on his clothes. Then stretched and prepared himself for anything.

'Well here goes nothing.' He stretched out his hand and muttered 'get off of me.' Nothing happeded at all not even a prickle of power from his hands that he had felt before.

Ah nuts nothing happened I wonder what you have to do to get something to happen.

Then suddenly out of the trees came a voice saying 'you have to think very hard about what you want to happen and than say any word you like because it is not the word but the thought that make the magic happen.'

'Who are you. show yourself.' Came Jeremy's voice whith a starteled skeek to it.

Out of the trees came a man like no other you have ever seen before. He was average built with black hair black pants and whereing black boots with a black trench coat. He had his hood up over his head so you could hardly see his face and looked very grim indeed.

'My name is Marvin and I can see that you have just learned the art of magic by choice or by acceddent I do not know but what I do know is that you are going to need a teacher someone to help you learn how to use it and how to do some verry usfull stuff that will save your life if ever you find yourself In danger.

'how do you know all of that and why can I trust you.' Jeremy said with hurried breathing and a pounding hart.

'Because of this.' Said marvin and then their was a bang and smoke filled the air as he and Jeremy were twereled faster and faster till sundely they hit groud again and they stoped spinning.

They were standing in a back yard fenced in with a six foot hedge. There was a padeo just ten feet infront of them and a pond ten feet to the right of them a garden ten feet to the left of them. They were in the middle of it all and what a wonderfull spot it was.

'where are we.' Jeremy said with a nervous twitch in his eye 'and how did we get here.'

'we are in my back yard and how we got here is by a teleportation spell that I know.' Marvin said as he shook himself out from the effort of it all.

'How far did we travel.'

Marvin looked over at Jeremy and said 'Oh it wasn't far maybe a mile to two.'

'So you live near where I live.' Jeremy said with a shocked look on his forhead.

'Yes just two streets over from your house.'

'Are there many of us you know, people that can make stuff happen out of nothing.'

Marvin said 'Yes there are at least a million of us on the planet. Come on lets go inside we need to have a lttle talk.

Jeremy followed Marvin through his side door and into his living room. It was the most odd looking living room you have ever seen. There were shelves of books with the most perculer names on them. Odd decorations like you have never seen anyware else. It was like nothing you could ever have imagined in your wildest dreams.

'I have never seen anything quite like this.' Jeremy said as he looked open mouthed at all the strange and mavilous stuff that was every where in the living room.

'yes it is quite the collection isn't it.' Marvin said as he walked in behind Jeremy he closed the door. 'I have been collecting stuff for many a moon to get it to this size though. I quite think that it is not nearly as big a collection as I would like it to be. That is besides the point though so if you don't mind lets move into the kitchen and get down to besness.' Marvin said as he swept Jeremy out of the living room and into the kitchen so quickly that it hurt.

Jeremy sat down at the kitchen table and waited for the old man to tell him why he was there and more importantly what he wanted to discuss with him.

The old man went to the other side of the table and sat down himself.

'So where should I begin, O yes I guess I better start by telling you that magic is a verry dangerous art to get involved in. Only the storng of mind and body ever survive long enough to do any real good in the world. So think long and hard at if this is sometiing you would like to learn more of and if it is I would be willing to mentor you in the fine art of magic.'

The old man stoped talking and just sat there with his hands resting on the table waiting for the response he was sure to get. He did not care how long it took to get a response because of how serios the question was.

Jeremy sat there and stared out the window to his right and tried to take in everything the man had said. He thought of his life before magic, how often he got beat up and all the problems that seemed to follow him where ever he went. He thought about how good it felt to get into a fight and come out of it without even a scratch. He thought about that he may not live long enough to do any good with this new talent to help the world. He most thought about what his parents would say about what he was getting himself into. It was too much for him he could not think straight, it all seemed so out of this world and could not possibly be true. He sat there for what seemed like hours but was really only fifty minutes before he spoke to the man.

'Why do people in this art not live long enough to do any good?'
The man responded as if his worst fears were answered.
'Well mostly because they get burt out. You see magic burns out the mind if it is used too much and in too high a dose.
You will not know it is too much or too high a does until it is too late. That is why most don't survie long after they turn twenty.'
He only told half of the truth the part he thought the kid could handel and nothing else.
The kid took that in and then said.
'if that is the only reason to fear the art then I am willing to take the risk because the reward are great. Even if I only last ten year at least I can say I have done something worth while.'
The man sat there for a while and then decided that right now the world despertly needed any extra help it could get even if it was only for at the most the next decade or so.
'Are you absolutely sure you want to do this because if you are not sure don't do it for I would hate to loose another one because there were not ready for it.'
'I am ready and I want to do it so just alow me to be mentered by you.'
The man thought to himself *I wonder if I realy should teach him but then again if I don't and hes the one that can realy do some good then I will be throughing away the cance of a lifetme.*
'ok I will do it but on one condition that you only try things that you have already learned.'
'Of course I will do it that way.' Jeremy said in a escited hyper voice.
'good.' Said the mans voice as he got up and whent over to the fridge. 'want a drink.'
'sure a coke would be good.' Jeremy said still dumbfounded that he was going to learn the art of magic by someone that certainly looked like he new what he was doing.

Mavin took two cokes out of the fridge placed one in front of Jeremy and one in front of one of the other chairs and he sat down and him and Jeremy drank there cokes in silence.

Chapter 5

The Mentor

Over the next coulple of weeks Jeremy went over to marins house on a daily basis and he taought him everything he knew and slowly be surly Jeremy was getting a grasp on his magic. He had learns how to communicate with any live thing and get them to do what you wanted. He learned how to manipulate matter to make food and drink for himself without buying anything. How to open up a pocket of subspace and put stuff into it for safe keeping for latter. He could not belive all the stuff there was to learn about magic and how hard it was to learn it. It took him one whole week to learn how to pick up a peable with it and keep it in the air. Mavin would say 'That's it keep it in the air your doing good maybe soon I will teach you to thorogh the peable next time.' Jeremy was always existed at the end of the days but he was having the time of his life and would not trade it for anything. He would take what he learnd at marvins house and practice it at home in the back yard at night just to keep his skills up. It was not easy but it was worth it because every morning he would have to show that he could still do the stuff he had been touhgt the previous day. If he was able to do everything just as well as the day before he would be taught some new stuff to try out.
He was not getting any time to do other stuff and hardly ever saw his family or anyone else for that matter but he did not mind this becase it meant he was not getting beaton up every second day or getting up to no good. He was finaly having some fun in the summer time and he was enjoying every mineute of it. He had not had this much fun since preschool and that was saying something.

One day while he was praticeing in the back yard he started to
sense that there was other wizards in the area doing magic but
he could not tell from where they were.
'I wonder who these other people are that are using the art.'
He wondered as he stood still in the back yard.
He dicided that he would go and find out and that is just what
he did.
' I will use a spell to home in on their location. And then just
follow where it directs me to.'
He started the spell and could feel the forces coming together
to find these new people. He started to feel a little tug to the
shouth east. He went though the house and out the front door
to the drive way then down the street that would take him in
the general direction that the spell was pooling him. He was
not in too much of a hurry he could tell that they were doing
something pretty big that would take along time and would
be going noware too quickly. Plus he could sence that they
were close anough that it was only going to take a half an
hour to get there at his present slow pace that he was walking.
He walked by houses with people out cleaning their cars and
kids playing in the yards all of them having fun and not
noticing him passing by or all the magic that was in the air all
around him and in the gereral area where he was heading.
He turned right down one rode and then left down another.
He cut through back alleys and through local parks. It seemed
to him to be taking a verry long time to get there but in fact it
was only half an hours walk.
On the way there he spotted his old feoes come striding down
the way and it looked like they were going to try and give the
beat down to Jeremy.
Jeremy stoped walking and got ready for their attack which he
knew was going to come.

They Slowley got to him as they walked down the road grining to them selves because they were looking forward to a good fight. There was seven of them all biger and what looked like tougher then him.

He just stood there waiting for the inebalble and was completely ready for them with all his defensive magic at the ready and itching to get used. He couldn't wait to mess with their mindes a little and get them back for all of the trouble they have caused the kids around the area.

He put up his defensive shiled so that nothing they could do would get through to him. He set it at mild physical force level of power out put so that he would have lots of energy to do other spelles on them.

They got to him and tryied to stat to pound on him and he made it look like they were making contact with his skin which they were not.

They ponded to him for five or so minuetes but all that happened is that he got a little dirty laying curled up on the ground and nothing else.

They stoped beating on him and got up and walked away. He got up and turned to them and shouted 'now it is your turn!'

He ran up to them and using a spell that made you super strong for short periodes of time picked up the leader of the group and through him into the ditch stomech first. Then looked at the rest of the group and said to them in a calm and meaneningfull manner 'who else wants a beating today.'

They all ran in every directing down the street and away from him.

When the leader got to his feet he did the same and ran till he could run no farther to get away from Jeremy.

Jeremy droped all the spells and looked around wandering if he could have stoped them a long time before this and made the hurting stop.

He thought 'aw well I guess I will never know now.' And
started down the street again for the source of all the power
build up.
As he was walking up the road he could sence that the people
were inexperienced and did not know what they were doing
and what ever they were doing it was getting out of hand.
He started running down the road to try and find where they
were and fast before it got any worse.
'oh boy I hope I get there in time because I think they could
blow up half a house with the amunt of power that there
using.'
He turned right down one street and left down another. He
ran around one coner to the right and there they were on the
left at the end of the street in the wooded area for the area.
He ran right into the woods and yelled 'what are you doing
your going to blow up this whole woods if you keep this up!
The group of three, two girls and a boy all turned to look in
jeremys direction. The boy was about jeremys age skinny,
medium hight, black hair blue eyes, wareing grey cargo pants
and a blue tee-shirt. One of the girls was a year older than
Jeremy brown hair, skinny, taller than normal, grey eyes,
wareing blue jeans and a white tee-shirt. The other girl was
about two years yonger skinny, short, red hair, blue eyes,
wearing grey shorts and a white tee-shirt.
They were standing in the middle of a clearing in the middle
of the wooded area. Doing a spell that was defently going
aerie.
'you know what we are doing.' The boy said to Jeremy.
'yes I know magic when I see it. I can do magic too.' Jeremy
said to them all. 'Let me help you. What are you trying to
do?' Jeremy tried to say over the noise.
'we were trying to form protection so that people would leave
us alone but it is not working properly.' The boy said in a
agervated way.
'I'll help you stop the spell so we can try again.' Jermey said.

He went into the circle and started to work his magic to rip
the spell apart so that it would stop. But something funny
happened they were all riped way from this space and flong
into nothinghness for the logenst time. Then they were
rammed to the ground so hard they all colaped to it. They all
looked around them in stunned silence. They did not know
where they were because it did not look anything like where
they had been.
'Where are we and how did we get here.' Jeremy said while he
was getting to his feet to have a better look around at there
sourondings.
'beets me where we are.' The boy said as he to got to his feet.
'and I surtanly don't know how we got here or how we are
going to get back.

Chapter 6

Dimentional Shifting

They all decided it was not safe for them where they were so they picked themselves off the ground and headed out to look for shelter and a place to think about what happened and where they were.

'So what are your names just so that I know.' Jeremy asked the others.

The boy answered interduceing himself and the others 'My name is Jack, the tall one is Marry, and the other one is Susen.'

'Nice to meet you Jack, Marry, and Susen my name is Jeremy. After the introductions they just walked on in silence for the longest time not paying attention to what the others were doing. They had traveled for over a hour when they spotted a cave off to the right and headed for it.

'We should be safe in here till tomorrow when we can try and find out what went wrong and how to fix the situation.' Jeremy told the others as they aproced the cave enterence.

'Stick close just in case and follow me.' Jeremy said while they were getting ready to enter the cave.

They all did as they were told and did not even complain that the new kid was bossing them around.

They slowly krept into the cave looking everywhere to see if anything was in there. They were half way into the cave when Jack said as quietly as he could to the others 'do you here something I thought I herd something like maybe breathing up ahead.'

'Stop I hear it too and whatever it is it is a really big something.' Jeremy said while putting out his hands to stop the rest of them.

'Back out really slowly as to not wake whatever it is up.'
Jeremy said as he could hear the something change position in
its apparent sleep.
But it was too late the something which was a black bear had
smelt them and woke at onece with a start. Streatched its
massive body from sleep. Got to its feet and smelt the air in
full and followed where the smell was comeing from making
almost no noise on his soft padded fure feet in the direction of
the kids. The only noise it made was from his toe nails on the
rock floor and his breathing in great deep breaths. It wanted
vengense on the creatures that had disturbed its peacfull
slumber.
Meanwhile the kids were slowly backing out of the cave but it
was not going to be in nearly enough time to escape the bear
that was on its way.
With in a few moments or maybe a full minute The bear
became visible in the tunnel. He was even bigger and meaner
looking then they thought he would be.
He roared at the top of his lungs and charged forword as fast
as his huge bulk could take him.
Jeremy put up a force field to try and hold the bear back but it
was no use the bear was just too strong and broke though the
field like it was made of wood.
All four of them jumped out of the way and shot stunning
spelles at the bear but they were not affecting him.
Then Jeremy did something that would be talked about for
ages afterword. He Jumed on the bears back and jabed his
hands into the bears eyes while trying to hit him with all the
power he could to stun him. The entire caveran lit up like it
was being flooded with light from everyware. The ground
shock from the explosion that followed the light show and in a
matter of a seconed the bear was out cold on his side and the
cave was collapsing all around them.

The others ran for their lives and Jeremy was not far behind them. They all just made it out of the cave enterance when the whole cave colapsed around them closing it for ever. The bear died instantly because of a huge bolder that landed on his head during the colapes of the cave.

Just then a wagen pulled by two donkeys pulled up to them to see what had happened and see if they were all right. The rider said 'To the gods are you peoples allright. That was quite the scene with the cave coming down like that. I ain't seen anything like that in my life. My word what a sight to be seen.'

Jeremy and the others got to their feet to look at the new comer weraly before going over to him.

'We are all right now that we escaped that cave and the bear that was living in it.' Jeremy said with a shudder.

'I would bet you are at that. Do you need a ride anyware?' The rider said.

'we are new around here and don't know where we are infact we are quite lost. We sure could use a ride to the nearest town.' Jeremy said and the others nodded their agreament.

'Well now in that case climb on board I can take you to my house first and then we can head from their to Mandederon which is the nearest city of any size. It will take us three days ride to get to the city I have to go their anyway so midest well let you kids come with me.

The four of them got in the front seet of the wegan and they headed out slowly on the rode to the house where the rider of the wegan lived.

'We should get to my house by night time Id emagin.' The rider said as they rode.

The rider was a tall mid thirties fellow with black hair, blue eyes, clean shaven, dressed in what would only be called peasent clothing of over two hundred years ago for us. He had carets and potatoes in the box of the wegan packed to the bim with them half and half. The rode they were on was not much of a rode but more a dirt track more like a loging rode then anything else. Their was trees lining both sides of the rode as far as the eyes could see. The rode was fairly strait but was not very flat so the wegan bounced around a lot making it verry unconfetble to sit on the wooden bench that was the front seat.